1. Crossing Home

CROSSING HOME

Crossing Home

The Spiritual Lessons of Baseball

JAMES PENRICE

ALBA·HOUSE   NEW·YORK

SOCIETY OF ST. PAUL, 2187 VICTORY BLVD., STATEN ISLAND, NEW YORK 10314

Library of Congress Cataloging-in-Publication Data

Penrice, James, 1961 —
   Crossing home: the spiritual lessons of baseball / James Penrice.
      p. cm.
   Includes bibliographical references.
   ISBN 0-8189-0675-8
   1. Christian life — Catholic authors.   2. Baseball — Prayer-books
and devotions — English.   3. God — Worship and love — Meditations.
I. Title
BX2350.2.P437   1993
248.4'82 — dc20   93-4222
                                     CIP

Produced and designed in the United States of America by the
Fathers and Brothers of the Society of St. Paul,
2187 Victory Boulevard, Staten Island, New York 10314,
as part of their communications apostolate.

ISBN: 0-8189-0675-8

Printing Information:

Current Printing - first digit	1	2	3	4	5	6	7	8	9	10

Year of Current Printing - first year shown

1993	1994	1995	1996	1997	1998

For my parents,
William and Nora Penrice,
a winning team.

CONTENTS

The goal of baseball
is to cross Home.

The goal of Christian life
is the same.

It is because of the Cross
that we can come Home.

Thus, in every sense
of both these words,
we long to be

Crossing Home

CROSSING HOME

FIRST, SOME FUNGOES

Come play in the field, and sing,
Sing to the glory of the Lord.

Marty Haugen

Baseball is a lot like religion.

Its followers put their faith, hope and love in uncontrollable forces in search of fulfillment and inner joy. They follow various "congregations" who play the same game but with different philosophies and approaches, and varying degrees of success. Sometimes the faithful get the results they want, and are ecstatic at the outcome. When events are not so desirable, some accept, some dissent. In the darkest times some lose hope altogether, while others renew the vigors of their faith. In good times, it seems everyone is a believer.

Baseball has more than certain structures of religion; it is rich in allegory to Christian spirituality. Its fans are blessed with a treasure of parabolic images which can turn this game, this gift to our lives from our loving Father, into a reflection of Him and the life He intends for us. As Jesus used the common events of everyday life in his parables, our challenge is to find God in the events of our culture and use them in new ways of evangelization. Baseball is ripe for the challenge.

As a Catholic, the superficial similarities between baseball

1

and my faith are strikingly apparent. Followers of each have much in common.

We both worship in a variety of temples, from ancient cathedrals revered as cultural landmarks to more modern sanctuaries of contemporary splendor. We canonize the heroes of our past and adorn our temples with icons to their memory. We print their images on cards and cherish them as sacred objects.

Our worship practices are both of a highly ritualistic nature. Though some elements differ with each service, others are quite consistent.

Some of the faithful arrive early to watch the sacristans prepare the shrine, while others rush in at the last minute. We stand as all-male clerics in colorful vestments proceed to the sanctum, assisted by youngsters in similar garb. Some join in the singing of the opening hymn, others simply wait for it to finish. We know when to sit and when to stand; not everyone knows how to behave.

Like the Church, baseball adheres to a liturgical calendar, annually renewing the cycle of life. We begin with the advent of spring training, where we joyfully anticipate the nativity of opening day. (This is a day of obligation in many towns. For some it is the only day of the year they attend services.)

We then observe a period of ordinary time, seasoned with occasional feasts. Among them are the epiphany of the game's royalty to a star-lit town to present their special gifts, and the transfiguration of the ancient prophets, restored for a day to their former glory.

Four months into the liturgical year many practice a time of penance, as their heroes tragically succumb at the end of a hard fought campaign. This is immediately followed by the new life of the post-season and the ascension of new champions to the throne. Left without our beloved in the winter of our despair, we are promised a comforter — the post-season awards, press tours and winter meetings — to sustain us until the dawn of a new liturgical year.

2

Baseball also has its sacred scripture. Psalms include such verses as "Casey at the Bat," "Tinkers to Evers to Chance" and "Take Me Out To The Ball Game." Works of prose, both historical and inspirational, are offered by the likes of Roger Kahn, W.P. Kinsella, Roger Angell, Peter Golenbock and George Will. Radio preachers such as Red Barber, Mel Allen and Ernie Harwell have contributed to the spread of the faith.

Baseball has also played a genuine part in real life sacramental situations. Couples have been married in ball parks during games. Marriage proposals have been offered on scoreboards, by announcers and on airplane advertising over stadiums. There are accounts of fans being buried in the uniform of their favorite team, the coffin lining embroidered with the team logo. In many families a child's first ball game is a rite of passage to a richer, fuller life.

I mentioned earlier that these are superficial similarities between baseball and religion. I've presented them in such a way that one might take them solely in a humorous vein. But just as in religion, the true spirituality of baseball lies deep beneath the surface of ritual. I invite you to explore with me beyond this surface, to probe the essence of Christian values which saturate the game and the institution of baseball. If you love God and love the game, come with me. I wish to deepen your love for both.

What follows are 23 meditations on various aspects of baseball and how they can enhance our Christian faith and prayer. Some of them deal with the intricacies of the game itself, while others focus on how we follow it as fans.

The capitalization I use will indicate allegorical references to various aspects of faith. For example, God will be referred to in various chapters as "The Umpire," "The Owner" or as our "Biggest Fan." "The Opponent" represents the devil and his forces of evil which seek to keep us from our Christian mission. "The Game" always refers to Christian life, and "Home," of course, is Heaven. Others will occur within the context of the chapters, as each new lesson is "pitched" to us.

I want to stress that in my allegories of God, I in no way intend to minimalize Him; God's role in our lives is so much more than that of an "Umpire," "Owner" or "Fan." These references are used merely to make specific points about God and His relationship to us.

So bring your cap, your pennant, and your binoculars. Buy yourself some peanuts and Crackerjack. Open your heart, lift up your soul, and let me take you out to the ball game.

EVERYTHING STARTS AT HOME

*It happened in those days that when Jesus
went out to the mountain to pray he spent
the night in prayer to God.*

Luke 6:12

Before a player can accomplish anything in The Game, he must begin by approaching Home. It is both the source and the goal of the journey, the starting point and the finish. This is where he prepares for his mission, receives directions, plants his feet, takes practice swings. While he must always keep Home in mind he can't linger before it, for his mission is to go forth along the basepaths, win glory for The Game and come Home a successful player. But he must always begin each journey by reverently approaching Home. He must know his relationship to it, approach it with confidence, and firmly guard his rightful place beside it. This is crucial in determining how far the batter will travel through the basepaths, and whether he will eventually return to Home.

How a player stands at Home is not important. There is no single correct way to stand when approaching Home. Players have their own way of expressing themselves through their batting stance. These stances are as varied and individual as the people who use them.

Some flap their arms or wiggle their fingers. Some lean on their front foot while others put weight on the back. There are open stances, closed stances, bats held high in the air, bats held just over the shoulder. Some wave their bat in anticipation of the pitch, others hold it steady.

The posture is not important. Though coaches will advise different techniques, each player must use a position most effective for him. What is critical in approaching Home is how close a player stands to it, and how tenacious he is in protecting his place beside it. For The Opponent on the hill will do all he can to keep the batter as far as possible from Home.

Some batters stand very close to Home as they make their at-bat. This is by far the best method. It is also the most risky. For The Opponent wants to claim a piece of Home for himself, and will do anything to discourage the batter from getting too close.

The Opponent will pitch inside to the batter who claims Home as his own. This often leads to the incidental or deliberate hitting of the batter. The Opponent hopes that the fear or pain inflicted by his attacks will discourage the batter from standing so close to Home.

> Watch out for attacks from Satan, your great enemy.
> He prowls around like a hungry, roaring lion, look-
> ing for some victim to tear apart. Stand firm when he
> attacks. Trust the Lord. *1 Peter 5:8-9*

The Opponent is happiest when he can keep a batter furthest from Home, for it is there that the batter is most vulnerable. The Opponent doesn't attack a batter standing far from Home; he doesn't have to. A batter with a timid relationship to Home is easy to deceive and manipulate through crafty pitches that tempt but do not connect. The batter's vision is much less focused the further he is from Home.

Distancing himself from Home, the batter is subject to the temptation of the curve ball, the slider and other breaking pitches. They look so good in flight, but on approach they suddenly move out of reach, usually just off the edge of Home. The timid batter is likely to swing at these temptations, connecting with nothing but air.

A batter who refuses to be intimidated by inside pitches and stands firm to his claim of Home is less likely to fall prey to The Opponent's deceptions. He will not be exempt from temptation, however, for The Opponent tries to retire everyone. He will be tempted by the split-fingered fastball, which stays over Home but makes a last-second drop beyond reach. Sometimes The Opponent can even tempt a player to hold off on a good pitch, making him miss an opportunity to produce. But a batter's chances are much improved the closer he remains to Home. His vision is much sharper and more focused.

> No temptation is irresistible. You can trust God to keep the temptation from becoming so strong that you can't stand up against it, for He has promised this and will do what He says. He will show you how to escape temptation's power so that you can bear up patiently against it.   *1 Corinthians 10:13*

The pains of being attacked by The Opponent don't go unnoticed by The Game. A stricken batter is always given a base as a reward for his suffering.

Yet despite the promise of reward, many players still shy away from intimacy with Home. They know The Opponent's pitch is still going to come, that it is going to be frightening and perhaps even painful. They want to be successful in The Game but are afraid to take those necessary steps towards Home. Their hearts are troubled because they know what they want but don't have the confidence to attain it.

> We believe in certain things about Christ and his message. We fail to believe in *him*.
>   *George Maloney, SJ*

We do not doubt Jesus, but we fear *our* inconstancy
and weakness.   *James Alberione*

Yet every star player, if he is honest, will admit to being
afraid of The Opponent's pitches. What's needed to persevere in
the face of fear is faith in the power of a close relationship to
Home. Steps taken towards Home without faith are too shaky to
accomplish anything.

When you ask him, be sure you really expect him to
answer you, for a doubtful mind will be as unsettled
as a wave of the sea.   *James 1:6*

For Home to be powerful, the player must truly believe
that he can reach base only by standing closer to it.

Though not seeing him, you trust him... your further
reward for trusting him will be the salvation of your
soul.   *1 Peter 1:8-9*

Not a hair on your head will be destroyed. You'll gain
your lives by your endurance.   *Luke 21:18-19*

Ultimately the batter never regrets establishing a close
relationship to Home. It is always the first step to getting on base
and starting his journey back towards Home.

Whoever believes in me, the works I do he, too, will
do. And he'll do greater works than these, because
I'm going to the Father! And whatever you ask for in
my name, I'll do it, so the Father may be glorified in
the Son.   *John 14:12-13*

CROSSING HOME

In my Father's house there are many rooms;
if it were not so, would I have told you that I'm
going to prepare a place for you?

John 14:2

The goal of The Game is to return Home to the origin of the journey. The batter begins a trek which will hopefully lead him Home to complete a circle of accomplishment. On the way he will meet many obstacles and challenges, and many attempts by The Opponent to stop his progress.

Once on the basepaths a player cannot wander about aimlessly. The Game prescribes a specific route to follow. Before a player can reach Home, there is a Trinity he must touch base with. Though the members of the Trinity are equal (each is Base), they play different roles on the basepaths.

First Base is the Father of the journey, from which all life on the basepaths originates. Second Base, being in the center of the diamond, assumes the role of Mediator, standing in direct line with Home. When touching base with The Mediator a player gets a clearer view of Home, and is said to be in scoring position. Yet The Opponent at this point still positions himself in the player's way of Home, so the player must also touch Third Base. Third Base is The Empowerer, for when touching Third Base the player receives an acceleration of power to boost him on his way to Home.

Though seemingly separate entities, The Three Bases of the Trinity unite as one pathway, the only pathway to Home.

When a runner reaches a point where he has touched all Three Bases, he often has to rely on the help of a Base coach to guide him safely to Home. The runner can see the goal in front of him but cannot always see the danger behind him which might cut him down short of his objective. At such times he must trust the vision of an experienced coach to steer him in the right direction, to tell him when it's favorable to advance and when it's best to slow down and wait.

As in any situation when we put our trust for guidance in the hands of another person, we can be given wrong advice. A player can be sent to score prematurely, only to be thrown out by a clear ten feet. Or the coach may hold a runner back in a situation where he obviously could have scored. Still, such decisions are impossible to make without some kind of guidance and support from someone in a responsible position. When a player has come that far he wants to be sure to reach Home; his decisions should not be made lightly or without counsel. Sometimes he just has to trust, then live with the consequences, whatever they may be. The Game does not fault a player for innocently following wrong advice from a coach, though he does have to live with the natural consequences. Occasionally he must learn the hard way which coaches are better than others; that does not eliminate his need for a coach.

No matter what the circumstances, a player can never reach Home purely as the result of his own efforts. The Game was designed as a team sport. The player needs his own talent and initiative combined with the help of his teammates, as well as other less tangible factors.

Occasionally a batter will hit a home run, circling the basepaths without difficulty and seemingly on his own merits. Such a feat is admired by the fans and great import is attached to it. Yet the home run was never a part of The Game's original plan — it emerged from the vanity of the players. (In the pre-Ruth era home runs were very rare. The Game called for speed and strategy. Many jumped on the home-run bandwagon when it passed by, and The Game hasn't been the same since.)

Two things should be noted about the "illustrious" home run. Those who try to win glory for themselves by swinging for the long ball are notorious for a high frequency of strikeouts. Also, home runs are never really as self-reliant as they seem. They depend on such factors as wind direction, pitch velocity and location, and the distance of the fences. (A home run to center in Wrigley Field is a fly out at Yankee Stadium.)

The Game's Creator didn't put much value in the home run. Neither should we. The majority of runs are produced through effort, risk-taking and communication on the basepaths. This takes the combined efforts of many.

> Don't try to go to God alone. If you do, he will certainly ask you the embarrassing question, "Where are your brothers and sisters?" *Charles Peguy*

Once a player reaches base, the success of his teammates will help him advance. So will the errors of The Opponent.

A player can take initiatives to help himself advance, and is encouraged to do so. But it is always in such instances that he arouses the most opposition from The Opponent.

Once The Opponent suspects the runner is attempting advancement he watches him like a hungry hawk. He'll try to keep the runner from advancing with many tosses and throws, trying to get him out before he can touch Base again. (For an alert player, The Opponent's throws bring the consolation of bringing him back to Base.) Once the runner does try to advance The Opponent is sure to be gunning for him. Often he has the ability to stop a runner short of his goal.

The Opponent is content to leave a runner alone if he

knows the runner is not going to try anything. Thus a timid runner doesn't have to worry about The Opponent's tactics. But he does nothing to help his own cause, either. Ultimately this hurts the entire team's chances of defeating The Opponent and winning The Game.

One very useful tactic for overcoming The Opponent is to combine individual initiative with the help of a teammate. When the runner moves as the batter swings the possibilities for success increase; so do the chances of failure. But if failure results at least teammates don't have to go back to the dugout alone.

Sometimes a player can walk Home, the situation is so obviously favorable. Other times he must slide to get in by a hair. Yet in the grand scheme of The Game both runs count equally, whether a player had it made all the way or had to barely get in under the wire.

> When those of the eleventh hour came they each got
> a denarius. And when the first ones came they thought
> they'd receive more, yet they, too, each received a
> denarius. *Matthew 20:9-10*

Further implications of this parable will be discussed in the chapter "Out of Time — The Beauty of Innings."

Some players enjoy the journey on the basepaths so much they forget that Home is the real goal. They get caught up in the glory of running the bases, the adulation they receive, the excitement of running, the thrill of competition. To them Home seems an abstract idea not at all related to the journey, a secondary consideration, something taken for granted. Many see the basepaths as an end in themselves.

But all the action on the basepaths is useless if it does not lead a player to Home, for this is the whole purpose of the journey. Once the player has tasted the glory of crossing Home, the glory of the basepaths seems as nothing. When a player fails to reach Home, the glory he accumulated on the basepaths proves no consolation to him, for it is no longer of any worth.

> You should have as little desire for this world as a dead person does. Your real life is in Heaven with Christ and God. *Colossians 3:3*

In the end, whether a player is safe or out at Home is completely out of his hands; the call is up to The Umpire. All the hard work on the basepaths gets a player in a position to score, but he cannot safely cross Home solely on his own merits. After touching all three Bases, he needs The Sacrifice to send him towards Home and give him the chance to score. At this point all the hard work, batting and base running skills no longer matter. The runner is at the mercy of The Umpire.

> Salvation is not a reward for the good we have done, so none of us can take any credit for it. It is God Himself who has made us what we are and given us new lives from Christ Jesus; and long ages ago He planned that we should spend these lives in helping others. *Ephesians 2:9-10*

> Then what can we boast about doing to earn our salvation? Nothing at all. Why? Because our acquittal is not based on good deeds; it is based on what Christ has done and on our faith in him. So it is that we are saved by faith in Christ and not by the good things we do. *Romans 3:27-28*

Yes, truly devoted players do have an ally when the time comes for the call at Home. In The Game, the Umpire doesn't call every thing by Himself; He has an Associate Umpire who works the basepaths. The Associate once traveled the basepaths as a player and had an out call reversed at Home. It is because of the

Associate Umpire's Sacrifice that all players can have outs reversed as well. The Associate Umpire will appeal on their behalf to the Home Umpire if they believe in Him and work with Him on the basepaths.

> For this is the will of my Father, that everyone who sees the Son and believes in him should have eternal life, and I'll raise him up on the last day. *John 6:40*

ARGUING WITH THE UMPIRE

...they challenged me and provoked me,
although they had seen all of my works.

Psalm 95:9

The Umpire is the ultimate authority in The Game. He has an expert knowledge of the rules and is better qualified than anyone to officiate. The Umpire is active in The Game but does not try to control it. He observes and makes judgments so that The Game can be carried out in an orderly and efficient manner.

But because The Game is played by human beings, it isn't always orderly and efficient. Chaos often occurs despite The Umpire's presence and quite against His intentions. Tempers flare among the players and fights break out. The Umpire's warnings about bully tactics go unheeded. Disruptive fans occasionally run onto the field interrupting play.

The Umpire sees hundreds of players' mistakes, but does not stop them from happening. He'll see that a pitcher is throwing too high to a power hitter, or that the infield is playing too deep in a bunt situation. But He lets the players make these mistakes that they might learn and grow from them. He'll enforce a rule that's deliberately broken, but when it comes to mistakes He lets the natural consequences take care of the correction.

If He stepped in every time a mistake was made, there would be no need to have players or a Game at all—The Umpire would do everything Himself. Players are important enough to The Umpire to be given the responsibility of actually playing The Game, all the time under His watchful, caring eye.

The Umpire does His best to be the presence of authority in an often unruly environment. Yet He constantly endures the arguments and complaints of players, coaches and fans who think they can do His job better than He can.

Consider for a moment the fallacy of this attitude. First, The Umpire has extensive knowledge and is highly qualified for His responsibilities. He has committed to memory the myriad rules of The Game so He can expedite a decision in even the most obscure situations. He has studied The Game and its many aspects more than anyone, and His knowledge is superior. He is more qualified than anyone to make a ruling in The Game.

Second, consider The Umpire's view of The Game. He is on top of everything. He calls balls and strikes inches from the catcher's mitt. He oversees base stealing from just a few feet away. He's right on the foul line to judge whether a ball is fair, and makes quick retreat to the outfield to rule on fly balls.

In short, The Umpire is the most knowledgeable and the best positioned of anyone in The Game to make authoritative judgments.

Yet a manager, positioned below ground level some 200 feet away presumes to second guess The Umpire, and to publicly show Him up. Players biased towards their own team also think nothing of protesting The Umpire's judgment, though at the time of the play they were busy participating and had neither the vision nor the objectivity to see the call properly.

Worse yet are the fans, several hundred feet away, who harass The Umpire for His performance. It is usually the furthest from Him who think they can rule on The Game better than He.

Everyone thinks he can do better than The Umpire, but few would voluntarily stand in His shoes.

How does The Umpire react to this anger directed towards Him? With remarkable grace and patience, and in a much more dignified manner than would many of us in His situation.

I used to think that if I were an umpire I'd eject a player or manager the moment they opened their mouth to argue. I'm the authority, I would reason, so they have no right to question my judgment. If they showed any dissent I'd get rid of them immediately. That would teach them!

I later came to realize how wrong my attitude was. That is not how our Umpire deals with us.

The Umpire understands the stress inherent in The Game. He realizes that participants build up a certain amount of frustration and anxiety as The Game progresses, that they need an outlet for these tensions if they are to remain emotionally healthy. The Umpire knows these feelings could ultimately inhibit the player's performance, and that would be more of a disservice to the player than ejecting him from The Game.

The Umpire also understands that at the root of a player's tirade is his passion for The Game and his desire to perform his best. A player only argues when he believes his efforts have not resulted in justice, and he defends his actions with a holy perseverance. Since The Umpire has a deep love for The Game and its participants He is patient with the player for his outburst, though it is an uncomfortable situation for Him. He would rather suffer the outburst than have the player not care about The Game or give up on it.

Occasionally a player's outburst will push the limits of respect, and The Umpire must eject him for his own good and for the good of The Game. He does not do this out of spite for the player; it's to teach him that while it's all right to disagree, it must be a respectful disagreement, and that ultimately The Umpire is the boss. Even in the case of ejection The Umpire welcomes the player back for the next game, and the relationship continues as normal. (That's why it's called "ejection" and not "rejection.")

When we are judged and punished by the Lord, it is so that we will not be condemned with the rest of the world. *1 Corinthians 11:32*

Don't be angry when the Lord punishes you. Don't be discouraged when He has to show you where you are wrong. For when He punishes you, it proves He loves you. *Hebrews 12:5-6*

Sometimes players wrongfully assume that The Umpire makes calls against them because He doesn't like them or as a punishment for something they have done. What kind of an Umpire would that be if that were the case! That would distort The Game from a fair competition where all players have a chance to one of favoritism where some players have no chance at all. The Umpire enforces punishments on those who deliberately choose to turn their back on Him and disobey, not on those who are honestly trying to play by The Rules but make mistakes because of their human weakness. Players must give The Umpire more credit than that.

Many times it seems a player's petitions to The Umpire fall on deaf ears, that nothing really results from them. Yet they're often effective in bringing about real changes in The Game.

If a player can skillfully make his case known to The Umpire, a reward can often follow. The Umpire understands a player's feelings of injustice (though the injustice may be a legitimate part of The Game the player does not yet understand). While The Umpire cannot change the effect of the call in question, He will often let another close call go the player's way as a recompense to him. Indeed, many times what seems to the player to be a curse from The Umpire becomes a later blessing if he handles the situation properly.

Thus we should try to say to Him in this situation, "Lord, you know I only desire to please you. You are free to correct me in any way you wish. But I cannot see where I have grown negligent or tepid, despite my sincere efforts to examine my conscience. So please make it clear to me if I am somehow failing you. Unless or until you do, I will not take seriously these vague doubts and anxieties." Such a prayer pleases Him immensely: far from being presumptuous, it is a strong affirmation of our trust in His goodness.   *Thomas Green, SJ*

When The Game is running smoothly many people don't notice The Umpire or praise Him for His efficiency. But when things go wrong He's often the first one they blame.

We must remember that The Umpire performs this thankless job out of free will and love for The Game, its players, coaches and fans. Consider that without Him there would be no Game.

Then be sure to offer Him your thanks and praise for a tough job well done.

NOT-SO-AVERAGE AVERAGES

Our weakness is the throne of God's mercy.

St. Francis de Sales

A ball player is considered a star if he can consistently hit at or above .300. A select few have attained averages over .400, but .300 is the norm for stardom. What this literally means is that for every three hits a batter gets, he makes seven outs. To put it bluntly, we make superstars out of men with a 70% failure rate.

From this point of view it's hard to understand why we admire these players so much. It is equally hard for some people to understand how God can consider them a superstar with similar or greater failure rates. But He does.

If we can cheer that man who seven times out of ten returns to the dugout a failure, then we can gain a small insight into God's all-encompassing love for His people.

Is the .300 hitter really a failure that 70% of the time he is not hitting safely? Sometimes he is. Yet what may appear to the world to be failures can become, on closer examination, actual successes to the true fan of The Game.

Consider what can be included in that 70% failure category. Bunting, grounding out and flying out to advance a teammate are positive contributions, but statistically they're recorded as failures. Sometimes what is clearly a base hit is erased by a spectacular defensive play of another, and is marked as a failure. But to the true fan these "failures," when executed in the proper spirit of teamwork, bring out our appreciation. God also appreciates our "failures," when they are the result of acts of good faith and love.

Especially pleasing to our "Biggest Fan" are sacrifices — when we give up personal glory to help out our teammates. In the eyes of some other fans and players such acts are considered foolish. But our vision is focused on the good of The Game, not on individual accomplishments. We sacrifice ourselves to help others reach Home. These sacrifices are great successes, though the world records them as failures.

A walk is not even recognized as an at-bat; indeed, it shouldn't be. The batter doesn't really earn his base just by ignoring bad pitches. He knows which pitches to avoid but does nothing of his own accord or initiative. Thus, even though he reaches base, in the eyes of The Game he didn't even pick up a bat.

So it is with God. It is not enough to just stay away from sinful actions — we must participate in noble ones, take a risk, swing the bat. We stand much taller in the eyes of The Game when we earn our base through effort than when we accept a "free pass" for merely looking away from evil.

> Faith that does not show itself by good works is no faith at all — it is dead and useless.   *James 2:17*

> "Since I was afraid I went off and hid your talent in the ground; look! You have what is yours!" In answer his lord said to him, "You evil and lazy servant!... You would have done better to give my silver to the bankers, and when I came I would have received what was mine with interest. Therefore, take the talent from him and give it to the one with ten talents, for to all who have it will be given, and it will be more

than enough. But from the one who doesn't have, even what he has will be taken from him."

Matthew 25:25-29

Even if we fail when swinging at evil, at least we're given credit for an "at-bat."

Sometimes players hit foul balls. These are honest mistakes which are forgiven by The Game, for they are not counted against a player in his average. But this doesn't mean that these mistakes are without consequences.

The Opponent (who thrives in foul territory) tries to catch a player's fouls and turn them into outs. Thus while the Game forgives mistakes, they can lead to irreversible consequences for all players. Thus care should be taken to consciously avoid them whenever possible.

God's forgiveness is so complete we might think it leaves nothing uncovered, nothing unresolved. When God forgives, what could possibly remain of sin?
The consequences!
The embarrassing results.
The pain.
The chain of events set in motion.

Commentary on Romans
From *The Way* Bible

One of the biggest problems players face is that they worry too much about their averages. They feel pressured by the fans to produce, and when they genuinely fail they get down on themselves. This is how slumps often begin. Players get into a self-destructive mind set brought on by fan and peer pressure.

But true fans love players unconditionally; it doesn't matter what the averages say. Even a .000 hitter receives the affection of a dyed-in-the-wool baseball fan. They love all players for one reason alone: simply because they're ballplayers. Because they translate the game from an idea on paper to a flesh and blood reality. Without even the poorest of players the game could not exist. They certainly deserve our love as much as the superstars.

> Insofar as you did it for one of these least of my brothers, you did it for me. *Matthew 25:40*

If players could only realize the unconditional love of true fans, they would not put themselves under so much pressure. Thus freed from their anxiety, they could use that energy instead to play the game better and in a more relaxed atmosphere.

If we could only learn to realize that God loves us simply because we're His people, we wouldn't put ourselves under so much pressure to excel. We don't have to earn God's love — it's given to us for free! We should stop worrying about what He thinks of us and just go serve Him, knowing He's madly in love with us.

> God is not a Shylock, demanding his pound of flesh for eternal life. In fact, I believe that, theologically speaking, eternal life has already begun in us because God's life is already in us. We should be celebrating this. We are the branches to Christ's vine.
>
> *John Powell, SJ*

Jesus said, "Whoever believes in the Son has eternal life" (John 3:36). He didn't say we will have it, or might have it. We already have it! The price has already been paid for our eternal life. Let's relax and live in it!

When our self-esteem is low we should re-read Matthew 25:40, but put ourselves in the place of "the least of my brothers." When we really feel among the least of God's people, this passage proves God's love for us! For even the littlest receive His love.

A batter can't put so much emphasis on his average that he's afraid of losing it for a greater good. One of our "saints," Ted Williams, entered the last day of the 1941 season perilously close to losing his .400 average. He had the option of sitting out that day's double-header and being assured of his place in history or risking it by playing in both games. He took the risk. He batted successfully, getting 6 hits and finished the season with a .406 average. Even if he had gone 0 for 8 in the double-header, he would have remained a hero in the eyes of the fans.

Just as we remain heroes in the eyes of our "Biggest Fan."

There is need of a daily effort to live in the present moment. To accept myself constantly. With all my flaws and all my sins. No matter what I am or feel I am just now. Knowing God who never changes accepts and loves me. *Bishop Patrick Ahern*

OUT OF TIME:
THE BEAUTY OF INNINGS

Timelessness. Among team sports it's an aspect unique to The Game. Players and fans are allowed the luxury of ignoring temporal limits and living free of the bonds of time. It is one of The Game's stronger attractions to its followers.

We all yearn to break free from the limits time places upon us. Time reminds us of our physical mortality. It makes us regret what we have wasted and worry over what to do with what's left. Time reminds us of our dependence on its cycles:

> A time to be born,
> A time to die;
> A time to plant;
> A time to harvest;
> A time to kill;
> A time to heal;
> A time to destroy;
> A time to rebuild.
>
> *Ecclesiastes 3:2-3*

In The Game time is irrelevant. We never have to watch a clock at The Game. Though each particular contest is finite, in the course of play, time is meaningless. Its duration is regulated not by the ticking of the clock but by the quality of the play. The length of innings varies depending on the players' efforts and actions. The players, in effect, take control of time by how well they make use of it. Time becomes subject to them, not vice-versa.

What an awesome phenomenon this really is. Just outside the stadium walls buses are operating on schedules, workers are punching clocks, kitchen timers are running, alarm clocks are being set. Yet inside these walls players and fans have crossed into a dimension where time disappears, where our finite world and the world of the infinite cross. What a lofty plateau that is!

As creatures of the eternal God we instinctively yearn for that plateau, where our temporal beings touch the timelessness of God, and get a small taste of what eternity has in store for us. This is the essence of prayer.

> In silent awe before the mystery of God we rise above the relentless pull of time — past, present and future — to enter the unchanging, uncreated energies of the Trinity. *George Maloney, SJ*

> Prayer is an intervention of God in human space and time; it is also the intervention (so to speak) of human beings in God's space and time. *Anthony M. Buono*

There is no better earthly metaphor for these statements than the timeless baseball game. For one precious afternoon or evening we leave our space and time for a taste of the eternal. This should be our focus every time we pray.

Yet the concept of innings offers more to The Game than just a sense of timelessness. This structure offers another benefit not available to participants in other team sports.

Trailing teams are never under the pressure of a clock to come through in The Game. Under most Game circumstances the phrase "too late" does not exist. Even if a team is far behind in the ninth inning there is always hope, for the chance of salvation lies not in how much time is left but on the quality of the play. Two out in the bottom of the ninth is never too late to overcome a deficit. As long as players have faith that they can get the job done, The Game will allow them to try.

The present is never too late to turn to God if our hearts are true and directed towards Him. Our nine-run rally may not come until the eighth inning, but that is not too late to come to our Father in a spirit of service. Jesus taught this in the parable of the workers hired at various stages of the day.

> Now when evening came the lord of the vineyard said to his foreman, "Call the workers and pay them their wages, beginning with the last up to the first." When those of the eleventh hour came they each got a denarius. And when the first ones came they thought they'd receive more, yet they, too, each received a denarius. Now when they received it they began to grumble against the landowner and say, "These last ones worked one hour, yet you made them equal to us, who endured the whole day and the scorching heat!" But in answer to one of them he said, "My friend, I do you no injustice; didn't you agree on a denarius with me? Take what's yours and go! I wish to give this last one the same as I gave to you. Isn't it lawful to do what I want with what's mine? Or are you jealous because I am good?"   *Matthew 20:8-15*

Unfortunately, some Christians use this "same wages" plan as an excuse for backsliding in their spiritual life. "If I get the same reward for coming in later," they reason, "why bother trying now? There will always be the 'late innings'." This is a dangerous assumption, as the following chapter will discuss.

FOR YOU KNOW NOT THE INNING

How do you know
what is going to happen tomorrow?
For the length of your living
is as uncertain as the morning fog —
now you see it; soon it is gone.

James 4:14

Baseball is subject to weather conditions. This presents players and fans with some unique dilemmas.

Ball games cannot be played when heavy rains are falling. If the weather is bad enough the game has to be called off entirely. Sometimes a contest begins, only to have the remainder cancelled by rain. Depending on how far the game has progressed, this can put an unfair burden on the trailing team.

If each team has had at least five at-bats, a game called for rain is considered complete and the score is final. The team that should have had four more tries to make up its deficit suddenly finds itself a loser without the extra chances they had expected.

When such instances arise, the importance of early inning achievement becomes painfully clear. Players who bide their time counting on late inning opportunities discover there's no guarantee those innings will be granted. It's too late to change their early inning actions when rain is forming puddles on the tarp. Since nine innings are not always possible, players must make the most of the innings they're given.

Our own lives are often interrupted after "five innings." Rain comes into our lives in various forms and we don't get all the chances we took for granted we'd have.

Even when we've made the most of our "early inning" opportunities, rain has a drastic way of slashing our present and reshaping our future. A loved one dies. We lose our job. A close friend moves away. We become seriously injured or ill. We thought we had four more innings and now we're facing what seems to be the end. We feel cheated, the victims of a Divine injustice. We demand our four innings, though we know we're not going to get them.

Yes, we lose our late innings sometimes, and consequently lose games. But while rain occasionally cancels a game, it never cancels an entire season. When we lose one game there's always another to play. And while we sometimes lose rain-shortened games, other times rainouts give us a fresh start later in the season. A game called before five innings is always re-scheduled. The teams get a second chance to play on a much nicer day; to get a fresh start in a much more conducive atmosphere. Rain has a way of clearing the path for new blessings if we are patient and trusting enough to search for them.

Two stories from Matthew use the image of rain to teach us we need not fear these times if we trust in Jesus.

> When he got into the boat his disciples followed him. And behold, such a violent storm arose on the sea that the boat was being covered by the waves, but he kept on sleeping. They came to him and got him up and said, "Lord, save us, we're going to die!" And he said to them, "Why are you afraid, O you of little faith?" Then he got up and rebuked the winds and the sea, and there was a profound calm. But the men were amazed and said, "What sort of man is this, that even the winds and sea obey him?"   *Matthew 8:23-27*

Therefore, everyone who hears these words of mine
and follows them is like a wise man who built his
house on rock. And the rain and the floods came and
the winds blew and beat against that house, yet it
didn't fall, because its foundations were firmly set on
rock.   *Matthew 7:24-25*

Even the games we lose to rain have their hidden benefits.
The time lost for playing can be used to evaluate our play, to see
how we can improve ourselves. We can catch up on items and
errands we have been neglecting. The rain nourishes our field
and cleanses our stands, and though it is currently unpleasant,
it will work to improve the conditions for the next contest.

Though we mourn what rain does to our game, we must
remember that it is affecting other people far worse. There are
people who have no shelter to protect them from the rain.
Sometimes the rain is so strong that floods result in great pain
and suffering. Perhaps we can use the extra time given us by the
rain to do something for those even less fortunate: to make the
rain a blessing in disguise for all.

For I was hungry and you gave me to eat, I was thirsty
and you gave me drink, I was a stranger and you took
me in, naked and you clothed me. *Matthew 25:35-36*

Rain can be a sacred experience. It can bring us back to the
priorities that make our lives truly full. Let us always be open to
the opportunities rain brings.

THE TOOLS OF IGNORANCE

Put on all of God's armor
so that you will be able to stand
safe against all strategies
and tricks of Satan.

Ephesians 6:11

"The tools of ignorance" has long been applied to the equipment a catcher must wear to perform the duties of his vocation. What an ignorant vocation it must be, many think, to don this awkward protective equipment and still suffer the pains inherent in catching. One would truly have to be ignorant to wear these tools when there are so many more glamorous, more prestigious and less painful positions to play.

The trappings of Christianity have also been considered by many to be tools of ignorance. Why on earth would anyone want to deny themselves, take up a cross, turn the other cheek, speak out on controversial issues, forgive wrongs, sacrifice, suffer? Why would anyone assume these burdens when there are so many more glamorous ways to live?

But where would a baseball team be without its catcher? His worth really becomes apparent when we examine all that a catcher does to better the lot of the entire team.

The catcher often decides what pitches to use to defeat The

Opponent. In doing so he has to deal with the varied talents and personalities of eight or nine different pitchers (many of whom can be quite stubborn and temperamental in their approach to The Game). He must keep one eye on base runners and be ready in an instant to prevent The Opponent from advancing. He must run to first base on every ground ball so that if a teammate makes an error he's there to back him up and prevent damage. The catcher must sacrifice his body in protecting Home when The Opponent is trying to invade. He must often block with his body a wild pitch in the dirt, to keep the pitcher's mistakes from hurting the team. (Yes, the catcher is often responsible for reversing the consequences of the mistakes of others.)

Simply, but most importantly, he must catch the pitches. Without the catcher there is no Game, merely chaos. The pitcher's offerings are useless unless there is someone there to back him up. The catcher keeps the game moving along, keeps it from becoming a meaningless farce.

This is what Christians do for the world. God pitches His love to the world and needs receivers to catch it and to keep the world from chaos — from becoming a meaningless farce.

Being Christian often involves many of the responsibilities of the catcher: the sacrifice of our person, pain, decision making, alertness, strength, energy, determination and perseverance. If Christians weren't willing to assume these as values for their lives, the world would be in complete and utter turmoil.

Some would argue it already is. In truth, much of the world is in turmoil, precisely because true Christianity has not been "caught." The values of forgiveness, commitment, love and justice have been pitched — they've just become "passed balls." If more people became willing to wear the "tools of ignorance" to catch these values, the turmoil in the world would be greatly reduced.

Then there are seeds sown on the good earth, which hear the word and welcome it and bear fruit, one thirtyfold, one sixtyfold, and one a hundredfold.

Mark 4:20

With a catcher a ball team wins some games and loses others. Without a catcher a team loses all the time. Some people consider the catcher's equipment tools of ignorance. Let's be thankful there are people brave enough and proud enough to wear these tools.

Let's be brave and proud enough to wear them ourselves.

Take my yoke upon you and learn from me, for I am gentle and humble hearted, and you will find rest for your souls; for my yoke is easy, and my burden is light.

Matthew 11:29-30

FROM THE PITCHER'S POINT OF VIEW

At this point I must make amends with pitchers everywhere. I have depicted them as "The Opponent," the evil force trying to prevent batters from travelling the basepaths in search of Home. I have characterized them as stubborn and temperamental, and as being totally dependent on their catchers. My allegories so far have all been suited to the offensive side of baseball, leaving out the essential roles of pitching and defense. In the spirit of justice and Christian unity, let's examine The Game from the pitcher's point of view: the role of team leadership.

The pitcher is truly the leader of the congregation on the field. He assumes all the glory and the shame that goes with leadership in The Game, the triumphs and the tragedies. He is given credit for both the victories and the losses.

Without the pitcher there is no Game. Without him the players have nothing to do. The pitcher is the one who receives The Ball from The Umpire and is responsible for delivering it to the batters.

> I've given them the words you gave me, and they received them and they truly know that I came from you.   *John 17:8*

What the pitcher does with The Ball dictates the course of The Game.

The pitcher faces Opponents constantly on behalf of his team. He is forever engaged in intense battle with them. His job, with the help of his teammates, is to prevent The Opponent from making progress on the basepaths, to keep him from claiming a stake to Home. This is an awesome responsibility not every player is strong enough for.

And strong a pitcher must be. He conditions his legs, for they give him strength to push off and put power in his pitches. He trains his arm so he can keep The Ball away from The Opponent's vicious swings. His shoulders, elbows, wrists and hips must be in excellent form, for as they move so moves the team's fate. He must keep his fingers strong and flexible to grip The Ball effectively. If the pitcher is not properly trained for The Game he will surely be hurt.

The pitcher has to use a variety of techniques. He must be knowledgeable of the strengths and weaknesses of The Opponent, and manipulate his pitches accordingly. Many times he tries to deceive The Opponent into swinging at pitches away from Home. Other times he challenges The Opponent to lunge at one right over Home, trusting his teammates to absorb the blow and throw him out. When The Opponent does reach base it does not always spell trouble. Trained defenses can eliminate two or three Opponents with one skillful play.

It is essential that the pitcher communicate with his teammates at all times. The Opponent will try to send The Ball beyond the players' reach so they cannot catch it. The defense must work together to position themselves strategically. There must be as few holes as possible for The Opponent to take advantage of. In an emergency situation where two defensive players are running for the same catch, one must take charge, or The Opponent's blow will cause them to crash and injure each other.

The pitcher is always in imminent danger of being seriously injured by The Opponent. He is perhaps more at risk than any other player. A sharply hit drive can knock out a pitcher in less than a second. With the responsibility of pitching comes great risk.

The pitcher's own strength is not enough to perform his job — he needs a foundation to push off of. The Game gives the pitcher one great advantage over The Opponent: The Mound. The Game elevates its pitchers above The Opponent so they will gain an edge over him. The Mound is where the pitcher gets his power; this gives his pitches more force, more effectiveness. From The Mound the pitcher gets a clearer view of Home and can be more successful in getting his pitches over it.

But The Mound is not enough; the pitcher still must be well conditioned. A pitcher can easily fall off The Mound if he has not adequately prepared himself for the job of pitching.

Pitchers have a lot of support from their team to succeed. They have not only the manager but the pitching coach, who helps him with his particular ministry.

Like Martha and Mary, the pitcher has to balance a life of action and contemplation. The work he does puts a lot of stress on him. He can't pitch every day. He takes a few days "off" between appearances, but these days are usually spent in observation of his teammates and The Opponent, charting pitches to see which ones are most effective in certain situations. If he were to work all the time he would wear himself out. All pitchers must know when to "seek the better portion."

Sometimes a pitcher fails in his mission, but when he does he's never left alone to collapse by himself. There is always relief.

Many pitchers have trouble accepting relief. They feel guilty if they have not performed 100%; they feel that they have let The Game down. Yet in fact The Game has relief designed into it, so the pitcher should take advantage of it if he needs it without feeling guilty. Everyone must accept his own limits.

A pitcher has an awesome responsibility for the safety of

the others playing The Game. Most of the time he relies on his skill to defeat The Opponent. But sometimes a pitcher will resort to violence by trying to hit The Opponent on purpose. When he resorts to such measures the pitcher is taking some severe chances. He soon learns that violence is often met with more violence. Sometimes a pitcher will hit The Opponent in retaliation for a teammate who was hit. This usually leads only to greater hostilities, bench clearing fights and even suspensions.

Sometimes pitchers take The Game into their own hands and try to play outside The Rules. They soon learn that lowering themselves to The Opponent's tactics leads only to injury, defeat and disgrace.

Most pitchers do an admirable job of administering The Game fairly and keeping its life-blood flowing. Our caps are off to them.

MANY TEAMS, ONE LEAGUE

There was a split among the people over Jesus.
John 7:43

Players and fans have many interpretations of how The Game should be played. Though they agree on several basics of what it takes to win, there are varied opinions on how to go about doing it.

There are many recognized congregations of The Game, and the faithful are divided among them. Depending on which congregation is followed players and fans will approach The Game with different ideologies.

Some feel a team should be built on speed, concentrating on base stealing and hit-and-run plays, bunting and sacrificing to reach Home. Others think power is the key, and rely on dramatic extra base hits. Still others concentrate on pitching and defense, believing that the offense will take care of itself.

Sometimes the differences in philosophy are relatively minor, and are no cause of friction between teams or fans. Other issues are more divisive, and are the source of fierce argument and debate.

For example, some people feel that heresies against The Game are practiced by certain congregations. The designated hitter rule, some believe, puts the pitcher's soul in mortal danger because it keeps him from approaching Home as his teammates are able to do. The rule's defenders claim this frees up the pitcher to concentrate more effectively on getting his pitches over Home and thus betters his chances of defeating The Opponent.

Another divisive issue is the playing surface itself. Many argue fiercely against artificial turf, claiming it goes against the spirit of The Game and causes injuries. Its supporters usually point to the economic advantages.

Yet another raging controversy which tends to divide followers is the question of how much input the faithful should have in matters of The Game. (Such as selecting The Game's "royalty" for the feast of epiphany at the star-lit town.) Some say the faithful have the right to choose their leaders. Others claim that the masses are not educated enough, and that such decisions are best left to the enlightened and knowledgeable; the faithful should accept their decision on faith. Some feel that the faithful should have more of a broad say in everything that goes on in The Game, since The Game was invented for them and affects their lives.

Some fans remain with one congregation their whole lives. Others switch when one congregation appeals to them more than the one they grew up with. Some people don't become fans until later in life, and adopt a congregation as their own. Some frequently switch from one to another in order to stay with a "winner." Some become disillusioned and stop following The Game altogether.

Players often change their congregations. When a player leaves one team for another his performance in The Game can increase dramatically. This does not mean that his former team was not good enough or that his new team is better. It simply means that for this particular player a change of scenery was necessary to bring out the best in him. In the eyes of The Game he is still a player as long as he is contributing positively.

But if a player leaves one team and does not perform well with another, it means a deeper problem is present and a change of teams won't really help. If he leaves one team only to criticize it once he's gone, he's not doing The Game any service but is helping to destroy it.

Some players change teams for very wrong reasons. Many times it's to make a personal gain without regard to his former or present teammates. Sometimes it's out of spite for the management of his former team or in anger towards its fans. If this is why a player is changing teams, the chances are he won't find real happiness with a new one. If he changes teams because deep in his heart he knows he can't play by the policies of his present congregation and will be a more productive player somewhere else, if his only motives are the betterment of The Game and his participation in it, his move may be a wise and beneficial one.

Yes, there are many differences among the followers of the game. But one thing unites them all. Though they have many different opinions, they all agree on their love for The Game. This is why The Game lasts despite differences among fans and congregations.

If The Game has survived for so long despite so much controversy and division, that must mean that division ultimately is not a destructive force. In fact, many times division can prove to be productive. Controversies have been effective in bringing about rule changes for the betterment of The Game. They've forced people to take a close look at how they view The Game and evaluate if there might be a better way to play it.

The ultimate goal of competition, after all, is not to be better than the other team; it is to become the best team you can be. On the surface competition suggests an adversarial relationship, but both teams are actually helping each other to improve through their mutual struggle. The Game is accepted as a beneficial element of society, though it appears to be divisive.

Even the founders of The Game competed among themselves. But they managed to establish The Game and countless mortals have kept it alive through the years, despite — and yes, because of — their differences. The power of The Game and the tenacity of its hold on its followers can conquer any trouble.

Under Christ's direction, the whole body is fitted together perfectly, and each part in its own special way helps the other parts, so that the whole body is healthy and growing and full of love.

Ephesians 4:16

DEFENDING THE GAME

You may as well know this, too, that in the last days it is going to be very difficult to be a Christian. For people will love only themselves and their money; they will be proud and boastful, sneering at God, disobedient to their parents, ungrateful to them, and thoroughly bad. They will be hardhearted and never give in to others; they will be constant liars and troublemakers and will think nothing of immorality. They will be rough and cruel, and sneer at those who try to be good. They will betray their friends, they will be hotheaded, puffed up with pride, and prefer good times to worshipping God. They will go to church, yes, but they won't really believe anything they hear. Don't be taken in by people like that.

2 Timothy 3:1-5

In recent years The Game has come under heavy criticism from those who don't follow it and from fans who have defected. They claim that The Game is old fashioned, out of touch with the lives of contemporary people. They point to other games that have more action, more glitz, more thrills that appeal to the senses. They say The Game is dying because it is not capturing the imagination of modern day society. They claim it drags on too slowly. They point to increasing fan attendance in other games and to the increased sales of their memorabilia. The Game, they say, is out of step with modern society and is in danger of losing its followers to newer games and pastimes.

What they say, of course, is true. The Game is out of step with contemporary society because society has stepped in a direction contrary to the spirit of The Game. The Game is timeless, created to last for eternity. The cultural trends of humanity are finite and transitory, merely "minding the store" until the next trend takes over. Society has kept but one ear to the eternal Game while following the world's temporary, lesser games. Each step towards these other games and each turn they require takes fans further from The Game. It is not The Game which is out of step with humanity — humanity is out of step with The Game. It is the world and its ambiguous ways which has crippled the fans' faltering steps.

Some of The Game's leaders have, on occasion, given into these worldly allurements. While some congregations have remained more or less faithful to The Game's traditions and roots, others have resorted to gimmicks to draw in the fans and keep them coming. Electronic or exploding scoreboards, costumed mascots, recorded music and sound effects, between inning contests and promotions and other such tactics appeal to the baser instincts of the fans while diverting their attention from the real reason they're at the park — to enjoy The Game. The Game should be the main attraction, but it often loses out to the high-tech gimmicks.

When fans begin to enjoy these distractions and come to accept them as part of The Game, The Game becomes diluted. In the eyes of the fans The Game is no longer what it was created to be, and this spells danger for both The Game and the fans. They become disappointed when the glitz and the glamour they've been accustomed to disappears for some reason, and all that's left is The Game. In such cases they don't know what to do with themselves, because their relationship with The Game has dissipated. They think they've lost interest in The Game when in fact they are suffering from withdrawal of the distractions which were presented to them not by The Game but by some of its misled hierarchy. Faced with only The Game, they feel lost.

But it is never too late to return to true love of The Game, to put aside the distractions and concentrate merely on The Game and its intrinsic beauty. The Game will still be there when the scoreboard breaks down and can't show the between-inning highlight video. The Game will still be there when the mascot has to call in sick. The Game will still be there when the sound effect machine can't make the "boink" sound at every foul ball.

The Game will still be there when all the fads surrounding it have passed. For in the end, we must face The Game by itself. All the distractions don't mean anything in the post-season if our team has finished in the cellar. And if our team has found post-season glory we'll remember that long after we've forgotten about the cheap gimmicks.

The Game lasts forever. Let's learn to love it alone.

> Don't let others spoil your faith and joy with their philosophies, their wrong and shallow answers built on men's thoughts and ideas, instead of on what Christ has said. *Colossians 2:8*

> Don't copy the behaviors and customs of this world, but be a new and different person with a fresh newness in all you do and think. Then you will learn from your own experience how his ways will really satisfy you. *Romans 12:2*

> This world is fading away, and these evil, forbidden things will go with it, but whoever keeps doing the will of God will live forever. *1 John 2:17*

Lord, who would we go to? You have the words of eternal life.   *John 6:68*

SCORECARDS, BOARD GAMES AND ROTISSERIE LEAGUES: THE NEW AGE INVASION

A campus chaplain at a Catholic university recommends crystals, the energy source of Atlantis, for personal help.

A Catholic women's college offers workshops in Wicca (witchcraft) and the goddess within. Astrology columns appear in the school paper.

...(A spiritist) addresses the widows' support group about spiritism at St. Peter's rectory.

A photo shows elderly Catholics with eyes closed, waiting for spirit contact with deceased loved ones and friends.

A Chicago parish hosts a professional astrologer to lecture on the stars and inform parishioners where they can go for further astrological consultations.

...A Franciscan convent offers "enlightenment" classes that include Wicca (witchcraft), I Ching (Chinese fortune telling), and oriental meditation.

The sisters staff "The Christine Center for Meditation," teaching Yoga, astrology and Tarot card readings.

...Catholic retreat houses and parishes nationwide offer enneagram workshops conducted by priests and nuns.

...I bought into many ideas and practices which are now termed New Age during my college years — and I regret it... I invite readers involved in the New Age movement to steer their way out of these deceptions as well.   *Mitch Pacwa, SJ*

The Creator gave us The Game, a field on which to play and The Rule Book. These are all we need. Yet through the years fans and players have invented their own tools to supplement those given by The Creator in attempts to enrich The Game. Some of these tools, like certain exercises developed by The Game's Greats, are quite helpful. Others, while on the surface appearing Game-related, are actually contradictory to The Game as intended by The Creator. Fans and players should be very careful about using these tools.

One tool many fans find useful is a scorecard. They place players in numbered categories according to their position in The Game. Players are assigned numbers 1 through 9. (Pitchers are 1's, catchers 2's, first basemen 3's, and so on.) These numbers are placed on a chart as a form of shorthand to track players' progress in The Game. From this shorthand a box score is generated, reducing The Game to a set of statistics "neatly" arranged and organized for easy reference.

Many fans enjoy using a scorecard, and in some respects it can be a useful tool. But some fans have become overly reliant on scorecards, inordinately obsessed with statistics. Though they claim to be following The Game through statistics they are really taking themselves away from it.

One of the problems of the scorecard stems from the fact that The Game is not played on paper. Players are flesh and blood people with complex souls and emotions. A scorecard is at best a very sketchy guide to evaluate players, for statistics don't tell the whole story. Fans erringly believe they get a true insight into a player by studying statistics on a scorecard.

Players don't always fall into neat little categories. Not all pitchers (1's) are poor hitters. Not all catchers (2's) are slow runners. First basemen (3's) are not necessarily tall and left handed, and shortstops (6's) can be power hitters. It would be difficult to categorize Pete Rose, who belonged to several numbers in his career, or Cesar Tovar and Bert Campenaris, who each were all nine numbers in one day!

The scorecard also puts players in a batting order, and suggests certain directions as the only ones players can take to improve themselves. A player batting in the 7th position, for example, will improve himself by moving up to 6th, and will deteriorate by sliding back to 8th. But who's to say batting 8th won't improve a player's performance by reducing the pressure on him?

We can't judge complex people by putting them in boxes with numbers. As we noted in an earlier chapter, The Creator doesn't judge us by statistics. Why should we?

Scorecards also trivialize the accomplishments of The Game. Picture this scene in your mind. There is a runner at first with one out. The batter hits a long fly ball to right, the runner takes off because he's sure it's an extra base hit, if not a home run. The right fielder flies towards the warning track at full speed, scales the wall, reaches over the fence and makes the catch. He leaps to the ground and fires a rocket to the first baseman, who catches it on two hops and steps on first to double up the runner and complete the double play.

Now here's the scorecard's description of the same play: 0-9-3.

When we reduce people to figures on charts we dehumanize them, and take away the natural luster given them by The Creator. Fans using a scorecard to keep track of The Game should be careful how much of a role it assumes in their Game participation. Light use of it may be helpful. Too much reliance can steer them away from what The Game really is.

Another practice many fans are involved with has absolutely nothing to do with The Game. It stems from a desire to be The Owner or The Umpire themselves.

> Shirley MacLaine writes, "Each soul is its own God. You must never worship anyone or anything other than self. For you are God. To love self is to love God." Remembering this inner divinity would solve the world's problems, as claimed by New Age educator Beverly Golyean: "Once we begin to see that we are all God, that we have the attributes of God, then I think the whole purpose of human life is to re-own the Godlikeness within us." *Mitch Pacwa, SJ*

The Game is played by real people under the direction of The Umpire. Many fans are involved in fantasy "games" where they try to be the Power in charge. Some of these games are played on boards using specially formulated cards which try to predict a given player's performance. Often they rely on the "powers" of dice and on the position of the "constellations" of dots on these dice. Other games are played with the statistics of real players, and fans pretend to be The Owner and make transactions as if they were He.

Fans think they're enriching their enjoyment of The Game through these practices, whereas these games are merely substitutions for the real Game. After all, they're not watching or playing a real Game at all: they're living in a self-indulgent fantasy. The longer they participate in these rituals, the greater the risk of being separated from the real Game and the graces it has to offer.

Some players rely on drugs to stimulate their bodies into an altered state, believing this will increase their performance in The Game. But this has the opposite effect of destroying their bodies, and making themselves dependent on man-made substances instead of the Creator-made Game. Drug use has led to the demise of many careers in The Game.

Many fans are also involved in predicting the end of The Season — worrying over when their team will fold in the pennant race. These things are not ours to know or figure out — let's just watch and enjoy The Game and trust it to take care of itself. We will contribute much more positively as a result.

There's no place in The Game for any of these human-inspired practices.

> Jesus said, "I am the way, the truth and the life. No one comes to the Father except through me."
>
> *John 14:6*

STAY TUNED

Christ comes only in secret
to those who have entered
the inner chamber of the heart
and closed the door behind them.

Thomas Merton

Those of us who grew up during the transistor radio era share a sacred childhood bond — the reverent practice of putting a radio under our pillow to listen to games past bedtime. The more ambitious of us in the Midwest would try to stay awake for games from the west coast. Many a morning I would wake up with the radio still on, having been lulled to sleep and comforted through the night by the gentle lullaby of baseball.

This is a childhood habit I have joyfully rediscovered in adulthood (though in this age of earphones, the radio no longer goes under the pillow!). Through this experience I have also rediscovered some insights into the value of contemplative prayer.

What a pleasure it is to turn off the light, tune into The Broadcast, close my eyes, and listen. Meditating and contemplating on the play-by-play, I get a vision of The Game meant uniquely for me. I know that thousands of others are also tuning into The Broadcast, but when I'm alone with my eyes closed absorbing its cadence, The Game suddenly becomes very personal; it has something special for me. No one else is interpreting The Game and its images as I am; no one else is receiving the same vision. Many are tuning into The Broadcast but it is affecting each one differently, becoming for each of us a private contemplative experience. Through contemplation of The Broadcast we each assume a unique relationship with The Game. As a result we become a stronger community of fans when we gather again at the park.

Though The Broadcast is available to everyone, not everyone takes advantage to tune in. Of those who do, not all give their full attention. Some are distracted by other thoughts. Some are engaged in other activities while keeping "one ear" tuned to The Broadcast. Still others find themselves "switching stations" — tuning into another broadcast when The Game is slow and tuning back only to catch the highlights. Some are interested only in the final score and statistics.

It takes effort, discipline and practice to put aside distractions and give our full attention to The Broadcast. We must not feel discouraged or guilty when our thoughts do wander. As long as our receiver is on and tuned to The Broadcast, we will reap the fruits of our listening.

> We should not, however, judge the value of our meditation by "how we feel." A hard and apparently fruitless meditation may in fact be much more valuable than one that is easy, happy, enlightened and apparently a big success... Certain temptations and delusions are to be regarded as a normal part of the life of prayer.
> *Thomas Merton*

> There are no techniques for producing the experience of God. He is the Lord of the encounter, and He comes and goes as He sees best.
> *Thomas Green, SJ*

True devotion to The Broadcast means the fan can contemplate The Game despite any problems which might possibly impede them. Poor announcers, static interference or a fuzzy Broadcast signal can still result in our reception. Only when we shut off the power are we completely isolated from The Broadcast.

Sometimes I still fall asleep listening to those night games. But even as I snooze the radio continues playing, lulling me so I can achieve a deeper rest. Even if we fall asleep during prayer, God who never sleeps continues His Broadcast to us, soothing us with His marvelous peace. We are His in waking and sleeping, in activity and at rest — at all times.

God works in us while we rest in Him.

Peter of Celles

As a child I thought there was no better way to rest than by listening to a ball game. As an adult I've learned there's no better way to rest than by putting myself into the soothing, loving presence of God and His 24-hour Broadcast.

Live in vital union with Christ. Let your roots grow down into him and draw up nourishment from him.

Colossians 2:6-7

THE PARABLE OF THE FREE AGENT

For you have been given freedom:
not freedom to do wrong,
but freedom to love and serve each other.

Galatians 5:13

Once there was an Owner who had 25 ball players. He held them under a "reserve clause," meaning that as long as they played The Game they were under His Ownership. In fact, He commanded that they have no other owners besides Him. He paid them all a fair wage; indeed, none of them were starving. Though they by no means possessed wealth or worldly riches, they had their basic needs provided for. Most importantly, they were playing The Game they loved for a very fair and caring Owner.

One day the youngest member of the team approached The Owner and said, "Mr. Owner, I feel like a slave. I feel I should have the right to choose another owner if I desire. Furthermore, I know there are more riches to be earned in this world than what you are paying me. Grant me my free agency, that I may go out into the league and earn my true worth."

The Owner realized the potential dangers to the player and to The Game if He allowed him to be disloyal, to seek other owners and goals. But He loved the player enough to give him his freedom, to allow him to go out into the league on his own to discover what will bring him true happiness. The Owner realized He might never see this player again, but He was willing to take the risk. He gave the player His blessing.

The player put his services up for bidding, and the other owners competed to buy his heart and soul. They made many tempting offers, each one trying to outbid the others. When the offers finally reached an astronomical figure the player accepted, anticipating the good life which awaited him.

Yet once he got a taste of a lofty salary, the player found he was never satisfied — he always longed for something more. So he signed an endorsement contract with a shoe company. He sold his signature to fans with incomes a fraction of his. He came out with a line of clothing and had his own television show. His fame and fortune exceeded his wildest dreams. Never under the "reserve clause" did he expect to be enjoying so many treasures. His days with The Owner seemed never to have existed.

Soon his fortunes turned, however, and the player experienced a kind of misery he had never imagined possible. While his previous Owner had been very forgiving of his errors, his new owner was not so merciful. With his unrealistic contract came unrealistic expectations from his new owner and fans. His new owner cared only about making money, and treated him as a mere financial commodity. He could find favor with his owner only for spectacular deeds, not for who he really was. Despite his best efforts he couldn't satisfy the owner or fans, and they turned on him quickly. The fans in particular became very resentful, since he was making so much more money than they.

He was photographed at a night club wearing the shoes and clothes of competitors of the brands he was paid to endorse. His contracts were immediately revoked.

The audience on his television show became so hostile that he had to discontinue it.

All the while the player found himself to be obsessed with

money, competing in an entirely new kind of game. Since he departed from The Owner several other players followed his lead, and were also being given large salaries. The player found that when another was paid more, he could not rest until his contract was renegotiated to better everyone else's.

All of these distractions diminished the player's performance severely. He was so caught up in worldly affairs he could no longer concentrate on The Game, and he became very unhappy as a result.

The Game, after all, was his reason for existing in the first place. He longed for the days when The Game was his only concern, when he could play it, live it, and love it without worrying about material affairs. He yearned for his former Owner who treated him with fairness and love, and who appreciated him simply for who he was. He decided to return to Him and beg for forgiveness. He wanted so much to get back to The Game, the real center of his life.

So he returned to The Owner and said, "Mr. Owner, I have squandered the freedom you gave me. I thought I was a slave under you, but out there I found myself a slave to money and possessions, fame and prestige. I realize now that in the simplicity of my life with you I had real freedom — the freedom to enjoy what is important to me without the pressures of worldly ways. Mr. Owner, I no longer deserve to be called your player. Please let me be the bat boy, and I will truly be content."

But The Owner called for the equipment manager. "Get a new uniform sewn for this boy. Get him some spikes and new bats. He's in my starting line-up from now on!"

Now the players who had remained loyal to The Owner were filled with jealousy. "Mr. Owner," they complained, "what's going on here? We remained loyal to you while this guy went out and made a fool of himself. Yet you never ordered new uniforms or bats for us."

"My players," replied The Owner, "you have been loyal

and true, and anything I can do for you I will. But this player who lost touch with The Game has rediscovered it, and that is reason for much rejoicing. Come and celebrate with us."

Moral: The fatted calf is the first to die. The lean finds the freedom to live.

LET THE CHILDREN COME, AND DO NOT HINDER THEM

Whoever receives a child such as this in my name
receives me. But whoever causes one of these
little ones who believes in me to sin, it'd be better for him
to have a donkey's millstone hung around his neck
and be sunk into the depths of the sea.

Matthew 18:5-6

Little League. The way we pass The Game on to our children. Nothing is more important to the future of The Game than how we teach it to future generations. We must not only train them in the fundamentals, we must also instill in them a deep appreciation, reverence and love for The Game. This is important if The Game is going to be carried on through posterity.

We must be very careful how we present The Game to our kids. A poorly run Little League program is indeed an offense to The Game.

Parents must keep an eye on who is coaching their kids. Not all coaches are competent or well trained, and should be observed very carefully. A well qualified coach should be supported unreservedly.

Some parents rely entirely on the coaches for their children's instruction. They reason that since it's the coach's job to teach The Game to the kids, they don't have to reinforce it at home. But what a child learns from the coach is useless unless he is able to practice at home. With no parental support adequate practice is not possible, and the skills planted by the coaches never get a chance to develop.

Parents themselves must show a love for The Game. If a child doesn't see The Game's worth in a parent's eyes, they won't develop a sense of its worth, either. They won't know the purpose of playing it.

The Game should be a family activity, where all members can find a common bond to enjoy. It must be something everyone can be enthusiastic about, not just something to do because one is "supposed to." To accomplish this, parents must find the meaning and purpose of their own interest in The Game and pass it on to their children.

The Game must be part of a total family lifestyle — it can't be a once a week activity. It can't be used only in bad times as a last refuge for family unity. It can't be used only in good times as a "special occasion" gathering. It must be omnipresent and all encompassing.

Parents must be patient when answering children's questions about The Game. They must not be upset when children make errors.

Parents cannot live vicariously through their child's experience of The Game. They must experience their own Game. They can not vent the frustrations of their own failures at The Game on their children's mistakes. They must not let their children lose heart, or they will never come to love The Game.

Parents should not only be active in The Game at their level but should do all they can at the Little League. There's always a need for volunteers when training children is involved. By helping the kids with their Game parents reflect its worth, as well as enrich their own participation in The Game.

Sometimes children quit The Game, and parents assume

guilt because they feel it's their fault; they did not do a good job of teaching and reinforcing The Game. At times like this parents must understand that not everybody loves The Game, despite our best efforts to foster that love. But The Game will always be there for anyone wishing to give it another chance. They will always be welcomed back. Parents must continue to love their stray children while continuing to love The Game.

Children should be allowed to try out many positions, to see all the opportunities The Game has to offer. They shouldn't be molded into one role but exposed to all The Game's riches.

Above all, parents shouldn't be upset if their child is picking dandelions in left field, chasing a grasshopper at short or lying in the sun in right. Remember, they're only children. And they're seeing and appreciating beauties we've become blinded to in our fervent devotion to The Game. The children have, indeed, chosen the better portion. Let them not be denied.

Keep all these in mind when passing on The Game to tomorrow's precious players.

And always stop for ice cream on the way home.

DISABLED LIST

Players of The Game get hurt.

There is no avoiding this. No matter how strong, well trained, or thoroughly conditioned he is, any player is subject to injury at any time. It's a risk he assumes and accepts when he signs on to play The Game.

> I'm sending you off like sheep among wolves; be as
> wise as serpents and guileless as doves.
> *Matthew 10:16*

Sometimes an injury will be relatively minor. Other times it will be quite severe. Once in awhile a player will become so hurt playing The Game that he will stop playing it altogether. Some leave The Game on friendly terms, others are quite bitter and resentful.

Unless an injury is very grave, it will not signal the end of a career. Many times it will not even interrupt participation. Dedicated players learn that often they must play with pain, and sacrifice convenience for the good of their teammates. As long as he's properly nursing his wound a hurting player can contribute without putting himself or his teammates in jeopardy.

But some players don't properly nurse their wounds; they grow more serious as The Game progresses. Either they haven't told anyone they're hurting or they simply don't care. Sometimes they ignore the pain, hoping it will go away. While they think that playing with untreated pain is good for The Game they are mistaken. It leads only to deeper interior injury and possibly the end of a career.

There is no reason for an injury sustained in The Game to advance to the point of being crippling. The Game provides plenty of support for its injured players if they avail themselves of it. The literature of The Game is filled with stories of miraculous cures, emphasizing The Game's sympathy for its injured and its desire for them to be healed.

> Large crowds came to Jesus who had with them lame, blind, crippled, dumb people, and many others, and they put them down at his feet and he cured them.
>
> *Matthew 15:30*

The Game employs trainers to help a player when he is hurt, to help him heal and to assist with recuperation. The player is put on a special list which insures that his spot on the team will be reserved until he's able to return to active participation. He continues to collect his pay, and is as welcome in the dugout as the players serving nine innings.

It is natural for a player to become injured because The Game is by its nature a conflict, and conflict necessarily involves injury. We are in constant conflict with The Opponent who is trying to defeat us. A player can let The Opponent win easily and thus avoid injury, but losing takes the heart out of the player. His natural instinct is to win. So he must risk injury to defeat The Opponent.

> You'll be hated by all because of my name, but whoever holds out till the end, they will be saved.
>
> *Matthew 10:22*

One of the most discouraging parts of The Game is that a

player often gets injured in a losing cause. He will sacrifice himself and his team loses regardless. On the surface it seems like a waste. But an injury, especially when sustained in a losing cause, has a tendency to pull the team together and make them a closer, more formidable force to be reckoned with in the future.

If players and fans truly love The Game no injury can keep them from playing or following. Only fear of the opponent can do that, and once fear takes control The Game is finished. A player cannot give into fear of either losing to The Opponent or getting hurt. Both are apt to happen. But The Game must go on for all those who depend on it and whose lives are enriched by it and love it.

For we know that if The Game is played with faith, healing is always available.

> A woman was there who had had a heavy flow of blood for twelve years that couldn't be cured by anyone. She came up and touched the hem of Jesus' cloak from behind, and immediately her flow of blood stopped... Jesus said to her, "Daughter, your faith has saved you; go in peace."
>
> *Luke 8:43-44, 48*

GIVE-AWAY DAYS, AND
PUTTING GOD IN THE BULLPEN

Not all the behaviors of those claiming to follow The Game are necessarily faithful. There are certain practices we are all susceptible to which do The Game a great injustice.

Some fans come to The Game only on "give-away" days. They are drawn by the prospect of getting something for themselves rather than by a desire to honor or absorb The Game. When no "freebies" are being offered these fans will be found someplace else. (Not likely even tuned to The Broadcast.)

When I was young such days at the ball park were few and far between. In Detroit we had only three give-away days, and they were all for children — ball day, cap day and bat day. I learned to love The Game for what it is, not for what it could give me. Not that I never accepted a freebie, but I was there more often on "plain-old-regular days" when all I received was joy.

Nowadays baseball caters to the materialistic instinct the world has instilled in its followers. The give-away items seem endless: radios, calendars, tee shirts, drink bottles, notebooks, beach balls, towels, seat cushions, posters, sunglasses. And an infinite supply of party favors. Often they're embossed with the advertising of the company which paid for these gimmicks, to draw people to the park and their attention to their products. This is called marketing, but it is not so much marketing The

Game as it is the materialistic values many of its leaders have come to embrace.

Just as many fans are found at the ball park only when looking for a "freebie," many people are found at God's feet only when they want to gain something.

When God is passing out graces these people vie for the first places in line. When nothing out of the ordinary is being dispensed they are distant and unmindful of Him. They'll come to God when they are looking for a bargain. But when they have to accept Him on His own terms they back away from The Gate.

What eventually happens to those freebies we get from the ball park? Their value is usually indicated with the passing of time. Many are stashed away on closet shelves, soon buried and forgotten. Many are lost or become broken. Few of these "gifts" eventually become a really important or esteemed item in the lives of the recipient.

In my own experience, these freebies don't stay cherished for very long. The free ball I received became lopsided after only four or five swats of a bat. A plastic mug I was once given melted in the dishwasher. A miniature autographed plaque mysteriously disappeared in boxes of "forgotten memorabilia." These give-away items lost their luster for me not long after I received them.

Yet for each of the aforementioned items I remember clearly the games where I received them, though they were played years ago. I remember the participating teams and the people I was with. Those memories became a permanent part of my life. The freebies were only transitory.

The same is true of the freebies which attract people to God. If selfish motives are all that are behind their approach, the attraction will not last long. God will still grant them the freebie, for He is infinitely generous with all His people. But if a freebie is the only thing someone is after, they will soon be disappointed by all that's involved in the offering.

> For the free gift of eternal salvation is now being offered to everyone, and along with this gift comes the realization that God wants us to turn from our godless living and sinful pleasures and to live good, God-fearing lives.   *Titus 2:11-12*

God hopes they will return, but gives them the freedom to decide.

If we keep our attention on God because of who He is and not on what He gives us, we will find Him much more valuable than any gift.

The same people who come to God only for freebies are the ones who also tend to put Him in the bullpen, calling on Him only in times of dire need.

Consider the dilemma of the relief pitcher. For most of The Game he sits in the bullpen — unneeded, unwanted, not called on to participate in The Game. If his team is doing well they tend to forget about him. When the team is in trouble he's the first one they turn to.

The relief pitcher usually enters The Game under one of only two circumstances. Either the team is losing and is in imminent danger of sinking deeper, or they have a slim lead late in the game and need someone to help them hang onto it. Both of these situations are very stressful.

No one calls on the relief pitcher with a 16 run lead in the third inning saying, "We don't need you right now, but come on in and enjoy the game with us." Sometimes God must feel like a relief pitcher. Many of His people leave Him sitting in the bullpen when things are going smoothly, and only "give Him the call" in times of trouble.

Yet like the relief pitcher, God comes through with His best for the team regardless of when He is called.

Ask and it shall be given to you; seek and you shall
find; knock and it shall be opened unto you.
Matthew 7:7

No relief pitcher would intentionally lose a game to show
his displeasure at being merely a mop-up man. Relief pitchers
are professionals and realize this is part of their job.

This is part of God's job, too, but it is not all of it. God wants
us to know He's available whether our lives are running fine or
are in time of need. He wants to be a part of our total life. When
we spend time with Him on the good days our relationship will
be that much stronger on the bad.

Even relief pitchers like to get a starting assignment once in
awhile.

EDEN REVISITED:
WHY WE WANT THOSE FOUL BALLS

You may eat any fruit in the garden except...
Genesis 2:17

The dream of every Major League baseball fan is to own an official game ball. People have literally risked their lives to retrieve this precious relic. (A man once fell out of the upper deck at Cincinnati's Riverfront Stadium reaching for a ball. Luckily his friends caught him in time and pulled him back to safety.)

I fulfilled that lofty dream (of getting a ball, not falling out of the stands!) at Detroit's Tiger Stadium the night of May 18, 1984. I remember the date because I immediately inscribed it on the ball with trembling hands. I learned from this experience that our dreams and goals are not always what they seem — especially when what we're reaching for is beyond our mortal limits, and when we reach for them with devious means.

I was standing with my friend Pat in the lower deck general admission seats in right field. In preparation for their game with Oakland, the Tigers were taking batting practice (a true spiritual experience not all fans take the advantage of attending). Pat and I were waiting, hoping that a ball would come our way and anoint one of us as the few, the chosen, the called. Suddenly Lou

Whitaker parked one in an empty section of seats about 30 feet to my right. There was nothing standing between myself and the object of my intense life-long desire. I wanted that ball so badly a frenzy overtook me. I lost all rational control of my actions.

Though I have no recollection of having done this, Pat swears that I did. I have no reason to doubt him. First, he wouldn't lie about a thing like this. Second, the expression on his shocked face confirmed that I had done something out of character and blatantly wrong. Third, knowing how berserk I felt after seeing the opportunity to seize that ball, I knew I was capable of doing anything.

The ball was to my right, its passageway unimpeded. Pat was to my left, myself being the only impediment to his path. As we both moved towards the ball, I swung my arm smack into Pat's chest and pushed him down into his seat. I ran for the ball in a maniacal state — I blocked out everything else. Nothing existed but that ball and I was destined to possess it. My heart was pounding, my hands shaking, my mouth dry.

Suddenly the ball was at my feet, and I reached down to grasp it. When I felt my hand surrounding that ball and knew for sure it was mine, I felt a surge of almost supernatural energy shoot from my hand through the rest of my body. I was finally possessing my idol, and I was letting the rest of the stadium know about it. People were actually applauding me in my idolatrous greed.

Back in the next section my bewildered friend was dazed, eyeing me with shock and disbelief. When I asked what was wrong I couldn't believe the answer. I had absolutely no recollection of having pushed him into his seat. I had been so involved in rapture I forgot my basic responsibility to my neighbor. What made that ball so important to me? Why is it so important to all fans?

Because it is, in a real sense, supernatural. Because it is from a major league field, which is inaccessible to us "mere mortals." The major league field is something beyond our natural limits, forbidden ground, something we yearn to be a part of but are not able to touch. When we get a piece of it we feel privileged to be a part of what is beyond us.

It is, from the point of view of The Game, receiving a piece of the Divine. We long to be a part of the Divine, and reach out for portions of it. We forget that while we have a valuable part in The Game, we are not yet called to be on The Field. We have been given all that we need to participate in The Game — we don't need to be reaching beyond the natural limits placed upon us by The Creator.

> Anyone wanting to get something in a supernatural way, as we stated, would as it were be accusing God of not having given us in his Son all that is required. Although in having these desires one presupposes the faith and believes in it, still, that curiosity displays a lack of faith. Hence there is no reason to hope for doctrine or anything else through supernatural means... now that the faith is established through Christ and the Gospel law made manifest, there is no reason for inquiring of him in this way, or expecting him to answer as before. In giving us his Son, his only Word (for he possesses no other), he spoke everything to us at once in this sole Word — and he has no more to say.   *St. John of the Cross*

> I prefer not to see God and the Saints, but to remain in the night of faith in contrast with those who are anxious to see and understand everything.
> *St. Therese of Lisieux*

In the book of Genesis there's a story of a couple reaching for a piece of the Divine. They were told they could have anything in "The Park" — hot dogs, popcorn, ice-cream, bobbing head dolls, souvenir helmets, posters and key chains — but to keep their hands off the baseball, for it was not meant for their use. Still they reached over the railing, and soon learned very clearly that having a baseball did not put them in the big leagues. We've been suffering because of it ever since.

In the early days of the major leagues fans were not allowed to keep balls hit into the seats, they had to return them. They were entitled to anything in the park except what was official team property. Until a "serpent" took issue and convinced a team to let him keep a ball he caught. We've been lusting for them ever since.

The roots of The Game teach us we're not entitled to game balls. The world has convinced us otherwise. So when we finally get a ball, we feel empty at not receiving the "Divine grace" we thought it would give us.

> The reason is that no creature may licitly go beyond the boundaries naturally ordained by God for its governance. *St. John of the Cross*

As for myself, my excitement about owning that ball dwindled quickly once I got home and put things in focus. My life went on, no different than it was before my "Divine encounter."

Soon afterwards I attended another game and was again watching batting practice. This time I had absolutely no interest in getting another ball. One landed in my vicinity, and I myself was knocked to the ground by a stranger running to retrieve it. I watched in amazement as 10 or 12 people battled in the aisle. "What's the big deal?" I thought. "It's only a ball."

How my attitude had changed. If I had not gotten that ball earlier I would have been envious of the winner of that battle royal (or would have been in the middle of it myself!). But after having acquired this elusive object, and after having hurt a friend to do so, I was seeing the situation in a very different light.

Fans must learn to cooperate with each other, not fight

over pieces of the Divine. They must accept their place in the stands and participate in The Game in the manner in which they are called. They must be confident that one day The Game will call them to take a much closer role on The Field.

Then they can get all the baseballs they want.

> Since you are so anxious to have special gifts from the Holy Spirit, ask him for the very best, for those that will be of real help to the whole Church.
>
> *1 Corinthians 14:12*

81

THE LIVE BALL

I never went to confession for that episode with the batting practice ball. Surely it was a venial sin, for it didn't meet the Church's criteria for mortal sin: it was not grave matter, was not done under sufficient reflection, and did not have the full consent of my will. I just went nuts! But while writing the previous chapter I realized that I still had that ball. It was still encased on my desk as a shrine to my greed, my idolatry, my vanity, my yearning for a piece of the Divine. Suddenly I felt the need to perform some kind of penance, to expiate my guilt and provide reflection for further spiritual growth. (And for avoidance of the "near occasion of sin.")

So I did something no fan in their right mind would ever do to an official, authentic Major League baseball.

I took it apart.

Yes, this sacred relic which most fans dream all their lives of possessing but never attain, that I was blessed with the privilege of owning — I tore through the seams with a pair of scissors and dissected the thing.

My purpose was not destruction, for I wouldn't purposely or maliciously destroy what comes from the Divine. Rather, as a constructive penance I directed myself to examine the intricate contents of this ball and to contemplate its structure, that I might gain some insight into the intricacies of my own Christian content.

The first thing I noticed as I opened the ball was that its cover was made up of two hour-glass shaped pieces of horse hide which are identical in size and shape. They interlock and complement each other to form a cover, much as male and female serve each other in complementary roles. (In fact, the terms "male" and "female" could well be applied to their insertion functions, as they are applied in electrical components, puzzle pieces, etc.)

Yet while together they serve different purposes, individually the male and female pieces are identical, equal, indistinguishable. One might say that in a baseball there is neither male nor female — both are equal in the eyes of the ball.

Individually, however, male and female serve no real purpose: they leave half the ball exposed. They are sewn together so that as a unit they can be a productive whole.

> And the Lord God said, "It isn't good for man to be alone; I will make a companion for him, a helper."
> *Genesis 2:18*

Though the seams that bind male and female are naturally strong, they can be separated, their unity destroyed. While occasionally the seams can unravel by themselves, the strong nature of their bond is such that it usually takes an exterior force to cut them apart. (Unless, of course, the bond was not sewn well to begin with.)

Inside the ball, nurtured by this male-female bond, I found a structure both amazingly simple and utterly complex. Immediately beneath the cover I found a thick layer of string wrapped around in a seemingly endless length. It was as thin as dental floss, and provided enough to clean my teeth for a year. Beneath this I discovered a tightly wrapped ball of dark yarn. Unravelling this brought me to a tightly wrapped ball of white yarn, concealing yet another ball of dark yarn. When I had unravelled all this yarn (and had enough to knit myself a good sized sweater), I found the innermost core, heart and soul of the baseball — a hard red rubber ball, about an inch in diameter.

That's all it was. A tiny rubber ball wrapped in yarn and string and covered with two interlocking pieces of horse hide. Amazingly simple. Yet the emotions and dreams of much of the world are captured by its motions, its travels, its fate.

How can hide, string, yarn and rubber so enrapture the imaginations and passions of multitudes?

How can hide, bone matter, muscle tissue, blood cells and organs do the very same thing? The answer lies in what is at the very heart of the structure.

At the heart of a baseball is the little red rubber ball. Without it, the ball is just a collection of string and yarn wrapped in hide, and does not make nearly the impact it does with its heart intact. Sure, we could use a baseball constructed without the heart, but it would be much lighter and less dense. Pitchers would find it harder to throw and batters impossible to hit for long distances. The rubber ball is the heart that gives life to the baseball.

Our faith and love of Jesus is the heart that gives life to us. While we could "get by" in this world without it, we, too, would be much less effective. A baseball without its heart will be beaten out of shape and eventually discarded. A ball with a heart can live forever. Christians without active faith will not last, but those with heart can live eternally.

Just like a baseball, we must closely protect our heart. That layer of string and three layers of yarn are very tightly wrapped. As a loose pile they were several times larger than the intact ball. We must keep our faith tightly wrapped, but not in the sense that no one can see it; in the sense that no outside force can invade and take it away from us.

No other ball is constructed in such intricacy and detail as a baseball. No other creature is created with as much complexity as a person. Our standing in the eyes of our Creator is a preeminent and special one.

Aren't two sparrows sold for a few cents? Yet not one
of them will fall to the earth without your Father's
leave. But as for you, even the hairs of your head are
all numbered. So don't be afraid; you're worth more
than many sparrows.   *Matthew 10:29-31*

It was painful for me to take that baseball apart. It was a
worldly possession that I had treasured for many years.

But I learned an important lesson through that experience:
by giving up a worldly good I gained a true insight into the
Divine. I hope I can make this experience a lifetime pattern.

Don't lay up treasures for yourself on earth, where
moth and rust destroy, and where thieves break in
and steal; lay up treasures for yourselves in Heaven...
For where your treasure is, there, too, will your heart
be.   *Matthew 6:19, 21*

ON WHOSE CONSTANT
INTERCESSION WE RELY FOR HELP

A boy lies ill in a New York hospital bed. He receives a visit from his hero, the legendary Babe Ruth. He asks the Babe to hit a home run for him. Ruth promises two, and delivers on his promise. The boy recovers, his spirits elevated by the special gift from his hero.

A young couple from New York want to marry, but the girl's father objects; the boy doesn't have enough money to support his daughter. If the boy can gather a proper nest egg the father will give them his blessing. The couple attends the Yankees' final game of the 1961 season, and the boy catches Roger Maris' record 61st home run. He is brought to Maris to return the ball; Maris tells him to keep it, and maybe make some money with it. The boy sells the ball for $5000, and his girlfriend's father gives his blessing for the marriage. They live happily ever after.

These are just two true testimonies to the special relationship between those who have reached The Game's ultimate plateau and those who are still struggling towards it. Testimony of the tremendous good that can be achieved through that relationship. Testimony that the delight is mutual; The Greats take as much pleasure in seeking us as we do seeking them. They want to be our helpful friends.

Some people think we have no business communicating with The Greats, that a true fan-Game relationship requires no intermediaries. But history has proven that many of The Greats have relied on other Greats to reach stardom; they become mentors.

> The Saints call forth other Saints. What brought about St. Augustine's conversion was reading the life of St. Anthony written by St. Athanasius.
>
> Eleven centuries later, Teresa of Avila will read the Confessions of St. Augustine... And Teresa's life took the turn which brought her to sanctity. Four centuries later, Edith Stein... became a Catholic after reading the life of St. Teresa, left her academic career in the university and entered Carmel.
>
> *Cardinal Carlo Martini*

Yet too often we think of The Greats and ourselves as existing in separate worlds where a relationship is not possible. We're merely in the stands while they're either on the field or already in the Hall of Fame. But The Greats are people just like us; they've merely advanced ahead of us to the mystical plane we too will one day reach if we keep faith. We are of the very same essence as they, we're just at different stages of The Game.

> You are strangers and aliens no longer. No, you are fellow citizens of the saints and members of the household of God. *Ephesians 2:19*

> It is true that there is, and there remains, a terrible veil between the visible and the invisible worlds. But it is equally true that love is stronger than death and that the love of the Risen Christ fills the heart and the life of our beloved dead. *Cardinal Carlo Martini*

Part of our problem in relating to The Greats is that we turn them into legends, causing them to lose the humanity they truly share with us. We need, in essence, to bring our ideas about The Greats "down to earth" so we can lift ourselves into their heavenly realm and truly share communion with them. We must identify with their humanity.

> The genius of St. Therese of Lisieux, the magic and really arresting thing about her is that she found greatness in littleness. Unlike so many saints she had hardly a single extraordinary experience. There were no visions, no revelations, no mystical transports, no miracles, no voices, no conversations with God... She lived in almost constant spiritual dryness... Her days were routine, as ordinary as yours or mine. Did God speak to her? Of course He did. He spoke to her in the way He speaks to us: through scripture very specially, and He spoke through the ordinary, banal, routine of everyday life. *Bishop Patrick Ahern*

While we should admire The Greats and communicate with them as friends, we cannot worship them. The Greats are not deities; they are subject to The Creator just as we are. Babe Ruth did not cure the sick boy. Roger Maris did not convince the girl's father to give his blessing to the marriage. But their interventions did set in motion the desired events, better than could someone of lesser standing.

> Indeed, while we can experience a warm friendship with someone still on earth, we still come up against our limits and inability to love as we would like. In our friendship with the Saints we are already able to experience ineffable and perfect communion with them in God and the peace of the Divine presence.
> *Cardinal Carlo Martini*

While we enjoy stories of miraculous interventions, like

those of Ruth and Maris, most of the gifts we receive from The Greats manifest themselves in more common events.

They're friends, they're family, they're our teammates. They're our role models, our coaches, our guides. We yearn for them. They wait for us. When we cross Home they'll come out of the dugout to congratulate us.

Let's not wait until then to meet them.

> We feebly struggle, they in glory shine.
> Yet all are one in Thee, for all are Thine.
> Alleluia!   *For All The Saints*

IT'S NOT THE SHOES

There was a cute television commercial a few years back that featured a small boy proudly buying his own baseball glove. After several shots of the boy dropping balls and missing catches, he was shown returning the glove to the store and telling the salesperson, "It doesn't work."

Ball players spend an enormous amount of time, attention and money on their equipment. They take pains to insure that their bats are just the right length, weight and shape, and are made of the finest material. They apply tape, pine tar, and rubber rings to the bats, and gloves to their hands to insure proper grip. Their shoes must have the proper number and configuration of spikes. Fielding gloves must be well-oiled and molded. Coal black under the eyes helps to deflect glare. Radar guns and video cameras record performances for later evaluation. Computer-enhanced imaging can pin-point every movement for instruction. Players rely on every man-made device to help them with their game. Yet without God-given talent, none of these things will help. All the devices and inventions of the human intellect can't compare to the talents and skills crafted by our Father. Everything must start with God and His gifts.

> For God in His wisdom saw to it that the world would never find God through human brilliance.
>
> *1 Corinthians 1:21*

Many people put their trust in human-inspired innovations rather than in God's inspiring gifts. As ballplayers know, God-given talent is the most basic and most important element for performance. Yet we look to our own ingenuity and creativity rather than looking for God. Of course our ingenuity came from Him, as does everything in the world. But we must put Him and His will first, and realize that without Him we can do nothing. Batting gloves do us no good if the bat is too heavy for us to carry. Let us rely on our God-given gifts and on the God who gives them.

> For men this is impossible,
> But for God all things are possible.
> *Matthew 19:26*

The television commercial featuring the boy and his glove did more than spoof our culture's worship of material goods. It highlighted the denial of personal responsibility so prevalent in our age. ("It wasn't my fault I couldn't catch the ball: it was the glove.")

How many other wrongs we deny responsibility for:

"It wasn't our fault she got pregnant (or we contracted AIDS), the condom was defective," instead of "We should not have been having sex in the first place if we were not prepared to responsibly accept the consequences."

"I couldn't help it, I was drunk," instead of "I shouldn't have let my drinking get so out of hand. Maybe I need help."

"Everybody else does it," instead of "I must live Gospel values regardless of what others think."

"That's not part of my job," instead of "I don't have to do it, but it will help us all out if I do."

The boy in the commercial was cute, but he was, after all, just a boy. Adults must accept the responsibility for their actions and take measures to avoid repeating past mistakes.

With God-given grace we can do it, regardless of the equipment we use.

STARTING IN THE MINORS

One cannot begin to face the real difficulties of the
life of prayer and meditation unless one is first perfectly
content to be a beginner and really experience himself as one
who knows little or nothing, and has a desperate
need to learn the bare rudiments.

Thomas Merton

Young players dream of stardom in the Major Leagues. They're attracted to the fame, glory and riches which come with celebrity. They dream of a quick ascent to the Major League level where they will live in luxury, basking in the esteem of adoring fans.

It's a wonderful dream. But there are many steps along the way most players don't like to think about when planning their careers. Everyone must start with training in the minor leagues.

No one likes to play in the minors. The bus rides, fast food, cheap hotels, and low pay are not what players expect when they dream of playing pro ball. Many players view the minors as insignificant, not really a part of The Game. They consider the minors a mere stepping stone to greater things. They'll work, but only to advance themselves and get out. They don't contemplate their time and experience in the minors as being valuable in itself.

Yet every stage of The Game is important, and there are important things for the player to do in each step. He shouldn't overlook menial tasks as being trivial, for everything done for The Game is essential to its life. His performance in little things leads to assignment of greater.

> Well done, good and faithful servant! You were faithful in a few things, so now I'll set you over many. Come into your lord's joy! *Matthew 25:21*

> Instead of scorning the small tasks, learn responsibility by doing them well. Then one will graduate to larger tasks. God will open doors for more ministry and expand our horizons of service.
> *Mitch Pacwa, SJ*

The Game gives us many examples that small tasks are not merely stepping stones to larger ones; that they're important in themselves.

> Whoever would be great among you, let him be your servant. *Matthew 20:26*

> For who is greater, the one reclining at table or the one serving? Isn't it the one reclining at table? But I'm among you like one who serves. *Luke 22:27*

> It wasn't that we didn't have the right to ask you to feed us, but we wanted to show you firsthand how you should work for your living.
> *2 Thessalonians 3:9*

> Peter said to Jesus, "Lord, why are you washing my feet?" Jesus answered and said to him, "What I'm doing you don't understand just now, but later you will understand." *John 13:6-7*

Naturally we want to be stars right away. We don't want to suffer the apparent indignities of the minors on our way to the Majors. Yet the minors are where the vast majority of The Game is played. There are infinitely more minor league teams than there are Major. More players toil in the minors than in the "Bigs." In fact, less than 2% of all minor league players ever play a day in the Major Leagues. We can't be looking to the Majors while we're in the minors; if we do we may never get there. The minors is where we are now and where we'll be most of our days.

We must accept all the banalities of the minors as our calling in The Game, and strive to perfect ourselves in our position and be always open to learning and growth.

> We do not want to be beginners. But let us be con-
> vinced of the fact that we will never be anything else
> but beginners, all our life!   *Thomas Merton*

WHEREVER TWO OR MORE
ARE GATHERED

One of the many beauties of baseball is that it can be played in its entirety virtually anywhere with the most rudimentary equipment. It doesn't require an ice rink, hoops, nets, backboards or paved surfaces. It doesn't need goal posts or a specially shaped ball. All that's required for a basic game of baseball is any open space, any kind of ball and some form of stick. It's incredible how many variations its "worship space" can assume removed from its official temples.

When I was in Catholic school we played in our parish hall on rainy days. The whiffle ball we used didn't have the same impact of a real baseball, but we still shared in the spirit of the game.

Baseball is played in backyards of every size and shape. Trees, stick piles, dried grass patches, leaves and a variety of other innovations are used for bases. Some families even consecrate a special section of their lawn for the exclusive use of the game.

The game is played on urban streets as "stickball," with parked cars and porches often being points of reference. It's played on farms, where cow dung bases make sliding a truly earthy experience. It's played in war zones by soldiers looking for solace in the face of imminent destruction. It's played at family reunions, company picnics, anywhere people love the game and feel a common need to share it.

When I first moved to New York as a naive suburbanite I was highly surprised and deeply moved to see a backstop constructed over a concrete playground in mid-town Manhattan. Even where the grass doesn't grow, the game has been brought and it has been loved.

No matter what conditions may arise which could possibly kill it, baseball perseveres because it burns in the hearts of those who love it. They keep it alive in spite of anything.

Neither does Christianity rely on physical places or tangible objects to survive, for our life in Christ is of the spirit and not of the earth. We don't need massive cathedrals or their earthly splendor. We don't need crosses or medals, candles, statues, icons or holy cards. While it's true these objects can supplement and enrich our faith, they cannot be central to it.

> What I condemn in this is possessiveness of heart and attachment to the number, workmanship and overdecoration of these objects. For this attachment is contrary to poverty of spirit, which is intent only on the substance of the devotion... Since true devotion comes from the heart and looks only to the truth and substance represented by spiritual objects, and since everything else is imperfect attachment and possessiveness, any appetite for these things must be uprooted if some degree of perfection is to be reached.
>
> *St. John of the Cross*

All we really need is the Word of God, Christ's Body and Blood and a loving community where that Word and Eucharist can truly live. With these basic essentials, Christianity can flourish anywhere.

It has survived prison camps, where inmates kept their sanity intact by reading scripture and reciting prayers. It's survived terrorists, who have murdered priests and ministers in the hopes of discouraging its propagation. It's survived communism, through underground parishes and seminaries.

Indeed, it survived its original, most direct persecutors who sought to kill it on a Cross. Because of that victory, Christianity can survive anything.

Wherever two or more are gathered....

THANKS FOR COMING.
DRIVE HOME CAREFULLY.

Grown men earn a very lucrative living playing a child's game. People of all ages invest considerable emotion, time and money following their exploits. Large segments of newspapers and news broadcasts are devoted to chronicling this little game. It has been glorified in art — from literature, painting and sculpture to plays and motion pictures. It has rallied civic pride and caused civil disorder.

Its terminology has saturated our language. "That idea came out of left field." "I struck out on that one." "Her speech was a home run." "They threw me a curve." "Did you get to first base?" "That price is in the ball park." "Take a swing at this." "Can you pinch-hit for me?"

Its brightest stars have been infused into our national heritage. Cobb, Ruth, DiMaggio, Robinson, Dean, Feller, Williams, Musial, Aaron, Clemente, Mays, Rose, Paige, Yaz, Matthewson, Mantle, Reese, Ryan, Seaver, Stargell, Brock, Gibson, Snider, Bench, Berra, Larsen, Maris, Kaline, Jackson. Any American will more than likely be able to identify most of these names. Give them another list of names from history — generals, presidents, artists, scientists — the rate of recognition would likely be much less.

We watch it. We play it. We dream it. We shout, jump, hug and cry over it. We've given it to the world. We've given it to our children. It's a driving, compelling force in our lives and we freely submit to its lure. We love it.

Why?

Most fans will be hard pressed to explain in words why they are so drawn to this game, why it assumes such a prominent place in our personal and national psyche. If this book has served its purpose, one reason should be clear.

Baseball is a reflection of our spirituality.

All of us are spiritual, whether we realize it or not. We're more than just a mere collection of biological parts wandering aimlessly on the earth. Each of us has an emotional, irrational, inexplicable spirituality which unites us to mankind through all eternity.

> ... we will continue to exist, provided we have food, proper clothing and housing, etc. But we have been made by the triune God to move to higher levels of being human through the mystery of faith which brings us into vital, loving relationship with the triune community of love... John presents us with a powerful, symbolic sixth chapter to lead us away from mere physical existence into the realm of the mystical, the world of faith which only God's spirit can open us up to.
>
> *George Maloney, SJ*

One marvels when reading literature from any age in history depicting the feelings and longings we all share today. Though bodies change and die through the years, human emotions live eternally from generation to generation. We are all connected by an eternal bond of sensitivity: our common spirituality.

None of us made ourselves; none of us were made randomly. We were created by an eternal, omniscient Being for a specific purpose. We all yearn, in one way or another, to know what that purpose is and to fulfill it as best we can. Everyone has a spirituality, no matter what they call it or how they go about finding it.

> Whether he or she knows it, every human person wishes to stay with God.   *Paul Hinnebusch, OP*

Baseball reflects in its very essence the nature of spirituality. It is people using their inner forces to compete with external forces. It is the bonding of community. It is sacrificing to attain goals. It is pushing to be our best. It is sadness at failure. It is exhilaration at success. It is going beyond limits, looking for new openings, diving and leaping for dreams, running in the grass, basking in the sun, putting our entire being on the line for what we believe in. It is returning Home from a perilous journey a tired but happy player.

It is life.

Needless to say, I've tended in parts of this book to paint both baseball and Christianity in flowering, idealistic tones. I've also tried to emphasize the not-so-pleasant realities of each. Though our hearts long for ideals, our minds realize facts. And the facts are that both baseball and Christianity have their problems.

Baseball suffers from the greed of both owners and players, and the resulting economic catastrophes. It must deal with substance abuse, violations in amateur programs, fan alienation, fights, controversial rulings, attacks from other sports, a biased news media, and the constant scrutiny of the worldly public eye.

Christianity must wrestle with the very same problems. Yet like baseball, Christianity will always be here. It is eternal, a burning flame not easily extinguished by cultural winds.

The Major Leagues may occasionally shut down due to a strike or lock-out. But as long as kids are playing stickball on some city street, the game will live.

Missionaries are imprisoned and killed for their faith. But

as long as one solitary prisoner is meditating on the Passion and forgiving his captors, Christianity will live.

Little League programs may run out of funds, but as long as there's one volunteer willing to organize a Saturday morning game at the local park, the game will survive.

The homeless continue to be turned away at the inn and to spend sleepless nights in dirty stables. But as long as there's one person to care for them, Christianity will survive.

As long as there are fields, vacant lots, playgrounds, streets, sticks, balls and kids, there will be baseball.

As long as there are people, hearts, souls, love, needs, compassion and concern, there will be Christianity.

There I go, romanticizing it all again. But maybe that's what Christianity is: to find the good in the midst of chaos and appreciate it, plant it and build upon it, while maintaining compassion for those who do not conform to the faith.

A friend of mine once explained why he doesn't like to watch sports. "The outcome will be the same whether I watch or not," he said, "so why be bored just watching when I can do something else and still know the results?"

He was right, and this brings me to my one distinction between baseball and Christianity. One fan cannot affect the outcome of a ball game. One Christian's involvement can make all the difference in the world. In life we can't afford to sit in the bleachers and watch — we must participate. We'll still have that high failure rate, get hit by pitches and foul tips. We'll be thrown out, tear our uniforms, fight each other for foul balls, ignore our friends in the bullpen, argue with The Umpire, be rained upon, become injured, and commit a multitude of outrageous sins, the consequences of which we'll have to live with.

But if we're trying our best, giving our sincerest heart-felt effort, our Biggest Fan will always appreciate us, and greet us with a standing ovation no matter what the outcome of our efforts. Our fellow players will benefit from the fruits of our efforts, no matter what the scoreboard says.

Lou Gehrig was blessed with one of the most sacred moments a ball player could ever experience. After a brilliant career as the Iron Man of the Yankees, he was struck with ALS, the fatal disease now bearing his name. On July 4, 1939 he was honored at Yankee Stadium, and he stood before a packed house to give his farewell message.

Imagine the holiness of that moment. Simultaneously reflected in Gehrig's eyes were the symbolic field of our earthly life and the real field of eternity. He was literally standing between our field of dreams and our Dream Field, our symbolic home and our real Home. He expressed his feelings at this awe-inspiring moment with this profound yet simple line:

"Today I consider myself the luckiest man on the face of the earth."

May we all be so lucky.

And may God bless you and keep you, and hold you in the web of His glove.

James Penrice
Staten Island, New York
December 8, 1992
Feast of the Immaculate Conception

BIBLIOGRAPHY

AHERN, PATRICK. *Therese: An Intimate Companion.* (Canfield, OH: Alba House Cassettes, 1989)

BUONO, ANTHONY. *Praying With the Church.* (New York: Alba House, 1990)

GREEN, THOMAS. *Weeds Among the Wheat.* (Notre Dame, IN: Ave Maria Press, 1984)

HAUGEN, MARTY. "Canticle of the Sun." (Chicago: G.I.A. Publications, 1980)

HINNEBUSCH, PAUL. *Come and You Will See.* (New York: Alba House, 1990)

JAMART, FRANCOIS. *Complete Spiritual Doctrine of St. Therese of Lisieux.* (New York: Alba House, 1961)

KAVANAUGH, KIERAN, and RODRIGUEZ, OTILIO, trans. *The Collected Works of St. John of the Cross.* (Washington, DC: ICS Publications, 1991)

MALONEY, GEORGE. *Entering Into the Heart of Jesus.* (New York: Alba House, 1988)

MARTINI, CARLO. *Journeying With the Lord.* (New York: Alba House, 1987)

MERTON, THOMAS. *Contemplative Prayer.* (New York: Doubleday Image, 1989)

PACWA, MITCH. *Catholics and the New Age.* (Ann Arbor, MI: Servant Publications, 1992)

POWELL, JOHN. *Unconditional Love.* (Allen, TX: Tabor Publishing, 1978)

The brief quote from "Commentary on Romans" from *The Living Bible* is from Campus Life Books, a division of Christianity Today, 1989.

The quote from James Alberione is from *The Prayers of the Pauline Family.* (Boston, MA: Daughters of St. Paul, 1991)